Meeting for Minds is a not-for-profit company whose main objective is to involve people with the lived experience of mental illnesses as partners in research into the brain and mental illness.

We fully endorse the underlying principles of LinkPADD relating to the management of mental fitness in the workplace based on the lived experience of managers and employees, and the need for their involvement as partners in research into this form of management practice.

—**Hon. Keith Wilson AM**, Director
Meeting for Minds

A refreshing dose of common sense.

—**Winthrop Professor Fiona M Wood FRACS AM**
Director of the Burns Service of WA
Director of the Burn Injury Research Unit UWA

I'm so excited someone actually wrote it all down…it does a REALLY good job of starting the conversation about high-performing teams but cleverly doesn't give enough information for a potential Driver to go off half cocked. It forces them to do a long-term, sustained program rather than just thinking they can buy a box of mental fitness…they won't finish it with all the answers but they will be armed with better questions. Great work

T0317354

—**Dean Crouch**, Principal Consultant
Resources Health & Safety Services
(Former WA Mines Inspector)

…………………bloody loved the book. I resonated with it immediately (the word 'Leadershit')…and wanted to buy the book and start the process straight away.

I believe the book is meaningful, and the main reasons were the real examples given in it. Every leader who reads this book will resonate with at least a few of the examples.

I had several favourite 'aha!' moments in the book.

As a qualified HR professional, I was interested in chapter 11. I agreed with all that was written in the chapter, and wondered how HR could assist in a POSITIVE way to influence and assist Visionaries and Drivers.

I also saw this as a way more intelligent form of 'Workforce Planning' from a HR perspective. If mental fitness were incorporated into workforce planning, it would mean huge gains for the business. This really excited me when I was thinking about it, and it may be a way for HR to be fully involved and take some ownership.

Overall this book made me want to be a leader in an organisation again—and I never thought I would say that!

—**Valma J Warren**, Director
Be Frank Results

We are more aware of mental health issues and are constantly reminded of the impact of poor mental health.

Very little has been done proactively to enhance mental wellness. This book is not only proactive, it is practical. The impact will be felt by all and will make a real difference to the lives of those employed, and to the business.

As a responsible leader, implementing the strategies proposed is essential, and right.

—**Steven Stanley**, Director
CEO Institute WA

I love what I read; I reflected on what I had done throughout my working career and it connected well with me. I loved the myths.

The book makes good connections from the Visionary to the workers, something I noticed to be missing from many places I have worked. I also liked the way it addresses workplace culture and how supervisors should conduct their business.

—**George Ray**, Retired Mine Manager &
Pit Optimisation Expert
OTML PNG

I have read the book (a couple of times) and really enjoyed it. I find it easy to read, with a good flow of information, not too many statistics, and some practical steps and stretches to work through.

—**Shane Stafford**, General Manager
Readi Recruitment Agency

I think it's great—I like the language and the way concepts are delivered.

—**Mark Paris Williams**, Managing Director
Donorcentricity (Fundraising & Development Agency)

This book has an uplifiting message for people working in institutions that have lost their soul. For someone who lost their daughter working as a junior doctor in the NHS it is a doctrine for humanity. .

—**Mark Polge**, Regional Medical Director
National Health Service, UK

The easy-to-read style presents critical concepts such as mental fitness, the Intelligent Org Chart (IOC) and the four scopes of leadership in a practical manner supported by numerous real-life examples. The Mental Fitness Stretch reflection activities and questions are a valuable way to personalise the reading and learning experience.

Implementing the concepts, developing an IOC, and working through the 10 Bands of organisational redesign incorporated within the LinkPADD system has the potential to create mentally fit organisations resulting in observable benefits for 'Companies, Teams and Self'.

Any organisation that is committed to its people and wants to increase productivity and profitability is advised to seriously consider the numerous advantages of LinkPADD. This book can be the first step in that journey.

—**Kathleen Zarubin**, Senior Training Consultant
RS & KZ Services

Kristopher G Harold | Alexis Ee-Khem Aw | John K Williams

MINDFIT

How to Create a Kickass Workforce to Achieve Long-Term Business Excellence

WILEY

To my mother, who struggled her whole life without ever achieving mental fitness and knowing the joy of work.

To Chloe, Ryan and Lucas, who have so much ahead and need to bring mental fitness along for the ride.

—KGH

To my accidental mental fitness instructor: Kenith, my son.

—AEKA

To our son Bob, a strong man with a kind heart. Keep fighting.

To our daughter Ashlee. Love you always.

—JKW

Foreword

I first had the privilege of meeting Kris Harold through my burnout research. He comes from decades of experience in management and mining operations, a world away from mine as an academic. In talking to Kris, it was clear that he wanted to make a difference to the mental health of employees in Australia; his passion for the topic was palpable. However, it was also evident that he had something new to say about how to make our workplaces healthier and thus more productive.

It is becoming more widely accepted in the field that organisations cannot afford to ignore the psychological health of workers. Productivity, employee engagement, absenteeism and workplace injury are all directly related to how 'well' a worker feels in their job. We know that neglecting to address these issues not only affects the worker who is suffering, but the organisation's bottom line.

This book encourages us to move away from the notion of mental health at work, and towards a new definition: mental fitness. The concept is relatively new and scholars are still in the process of defining the term. However, the benefits of the term 'mental fitness' are widely recognised and, in exploring the notion, this book encourages us to think about what is strong, rather than merely what is wrong. The term 'mental fitness' diminishes the stigma that plagues the term 'mental health'. And finally, it allows managers to see the psychological health of employees as an occupational imperative that is just as important as preventing physical illness and injury on the job.

The authors move beyond the more obvious strategies to achieve psychological wellbeing in the workplace, and dig a little deeper, exploring culture, attitudes, values and self-awareness for managers. It is a book that will help managers assess themselves and their organisation honestly, and diagnose issues that need to be addressed in order to achieve mental fitness. We know that managers are the first line of defence in safeguarding the wellbeing of staff. Read this book if you want to be a better manager, have a more productive team and improve the working lives of your employees.

Dr Marieke Ledingham
University of Notre Dame, Australia

Contents

About the authors

Kristopher G. Harold

- Founder, LinkPADD
- workplace futurist and org design and development specialist
- AIM WA Leader of the Year Award (Finalist 2015)
- Lean Six Sigma Black Belt

With ten-plus years of senior management experience, Kris has applied his unique way of addressing peak performance in the workplace with transformational results by introducing LinkPADD and the Link:Flow:Grow methodology. Companies in the transport, mining, manufacturing and construction industries have been part of the development journey since 2012. Kris is a graduate of both UWA (Science of Human Performance) and Curtin (Business) and a keen proponent of mental fitness in the workplace in an industry where mental health issues cost an average worksite of 170 employees $300 000 to $400 000 per year. The Intelligent Org Chart he conceptualised sets the foundation for the individuals, teams and departments of an organisation to perform at their EveryBest. Kris has learnt across both corporate and family businesses that the philosophy of 'Mental Fitness First' ensures managers are equipped with the personal and organisational skills to facilitate a sustainable culture of success.

John K. Williams

- Director, Combined Team Services
- Project Director, LinkPADD
- Workplace Systems and Business Performance coach
- Facilitator, Click! Colours

Unlike many trainers or coaches, John has been a supervisor and manager with personal insights into the issues facing his clients' frontline managers, and what they need to succeed. Having served for 20 years as an organisational design and development coach, John has worked with thousands of groups, from the smallest of businesses to the biggest resource industry players. He has written many business management documents and training materials for blue-collar frontline managers and developed nationally accredited courses and qualifications. His presentations have been well received at work groups, conferences and industry events. Before running his own business, John did the hard yards in his early career and worked his way up into positions of responsibility and accountability, building his capabilities along the way. He has always seen people as the key to success, and has the expertise to help organisations create a mentally fit workplace culture that maximises the wellbeing of their people to create outstanding business outcomes.

Alexis Ee-Khem Aw

- Word Alchemist—turning words into gold to let your business shine
- Marketing Communicator, LinkPADD
- communications specialist, copywriter, copy coach, wellness facilitator
- Master of Arts, Communication Management (UniSA)

Alexis is a writer acknowledged by Kris and John as a co-author who articulates their boldly innovative and humane system of change management, and transforms their beehive of complex ideas into a light and engaging read. Alexis's input distils the essence and authenticity of Kris and John's gritty and disruptive approach to organisational design and development for easy sharing. She had the most fun spinning their field encounters into stories and suggesting new terminology for key concepts. What she finds most fulfilling is the privilege of being the one who gets to capture Kris and John's managerial genius on paper for posterity.

Acknowledgements

The inspiration

The authors would like to acknowledge two fantastically supportive and inspirational people who care deeply about the lived experience of mental health, and lead important research in Australia and overseas.

The Honourable Keith Wilson and Maria Halphen are directors of Meeting for Minds, a multinational not-for-profit organisation that involves people with lived experience of mental illness as partners in the planning and understanding of research into the brain and disorders of the brain. This approach directly adds value to research and discernible benefits for those with hard-to-treat psychotic and mood disorders.

Keith is a former Western Australian minister for health, and chairman of the Mental Health Council of Australia. He is keenly interested in organisations improving the wellbeing of all employees.

Maria is committed to enhancing research in the field of mental health, particular international research. She founded Meeting for Minds in order to improve the lives of people living with serious mental illness. Maria is also the founding president of the Philippe & Maria Halphen Foundation, based in Paris, France, under the auspices of the French Academy of Science.

Without their guidance and support, pushing through the barriers in organisational mental fitness would have been so much harder.

The reviewers

The authors are also delighted at the enthusiastic and brilliantly constructive feedback we received from our first wave of reviewers: Bryn Jones, Dean Crouch, Frank Henderson, George Ray, Hon. Keith Wilson, Jamie Pirie, Jeanette Denham, Kathleen Zarubin, Mark Paris Williams, Mark Polge, Professor Fiona M Wood, Shane Stafford, Steven Stanley, and the inimitable Valma J Warren. We are also appreciative of Professor Gary Martin's permission to use content from the Australian Institute of Management Education & Training (AIM).

The publishing team

The authors are extremely grateful to Senior Commissioning Editor Lucy Raymond at John Wiley and Sons for accepting our fledgling book proposal and initial 25 000-word manuscript. We appreciate the masterful way Sandra Balonyi orchestrated a structural edit from Melbourne (essentially transforming our literary caterpillar into a butterfly) and helped us realise that 'workplace mental fitness' was a more accurate term than 'organisational mental fitness'. We respect the magnificent precision with which Canadian-based copy editor Allison Hiew brought us to the editorial finish line like a personal trainer beefing us up to be heavyweight authors worthy of Wiley. Senior Editor Ingrid Bond was indispensable in managing our first major book project like a pro, especially in collaborating with us to evolve the book title and subtitle.

The trailblazers

PricewaterhouseCoopers (PwC) is consistently ranked number one as a Big Four auditor and the top company Australians want to work for. It is a privilege and honour to be working with thought leaders Ross Thorpe, Penelope Harris and Graeme Hartnett in a collaboration made in heaven.

Preface

Billions of dollars are wasted annually across Australia.

In the world of work, poor mental health and wellbeing exact a tremendous cost to industries. Work stress and burnout fuel a loss of billions of dollars:

- **$11 billion** per year is lost Australia-wide through absenteeism ($4.7 billion), presenteeism ($6.1 billion) and compensation claims ($146 million), estimates a 2014 PricewaterhouseCoopers (PwC) study.[1]

- **$718 million** was lost in all stress-related claims in Western Australia in 2015–16 alone according to WorkCover WA, reflecting a **25 per cent increase** over four years.[2]

- In 2015, the Minerals Council of Australia found that **$320 million to $450 million** is lost to mental health issues in the resource industry every year (this means $300 000 to $400 000 for an average worksite of 170 people).[3]

Nobody should be getting hurt, mentally or physically, on the job.

The numbers tell us that the current focus on mental health is not improving worker wellbeing. Ironically, it's causing increased stress and job insecurity.

There are complex problems in businesses of every kind that current management theories have not yet solved. This is because everyone is trying to fix mental *health* issues in the workplace without first addressing a foundational issue—the lack of workplace mental *fitness*.

I (Kris) wish I had been taught the key components of mental fitness earlier in my life. I believe this would have made me a better manager, father, son and husband.

Fortunately, in the ten years I've led large enterprises in the mining, manufacturing, transport and construction industries, I figured something out that helped me produce results such as these:

- 90 per cent reduction in workplace safety incidents in an organisation with 450 staff
- up to 48 per cent decrease in workers compensation premiums per annum in an organisation with 190 staff
- 30 per cent to 50 per cent improvement in productivity and quality in organisations with teams of tens to hundreds of people
- transformation of a high staff turnover (value leaching) workplace to zero staff turnover.

Yes, you heard right: **zero staff turnover**.

Remember the old adage: people don't leave the company, they leave their manager. When the manager gets it right then nobody leaves. (Unless they leave to pursue personal goals, which isn't negative staff turnover but positive life progress.)

In writing this book, I want to share a perspective and system that I truly hope can improve your work life. The system is called Link:Flow:Grow. It will provide the missing MindFit link that will show you how to create a kickass workforce to achieve long-term business excellence.

It doesn't matter if you are a senior or junior manager, white-collar or blue-collar worker. I know our program has empowered many people I've worked with, and wish the same for you: in your Company, your Team and your Self (CTS).

Remember 'CTS', because change has to happen at all three levels: Company, Team and Self. Also because CTS is the acronym for my co-author John's training and workforce development business (Combined Team Services), which has been instrumental in helping me achieve what I have as a manager.

As a senior manager, I see too often that leaders put other priorities above mental health and mental fitness. Conditioned left-brain thinking puts these concerns at the back of the line.

Mental health experts are very clear in recommending goals but, judging by the results, neither they nor business leaders know exactly what needs to be done, and how. It's complicated.

You'll read more about mental fitness further along in the book. For now, keep in mind that the work of managers and mental health professionals may interact but are not the same.

I'll stick to talking about what I know best: workplace mental fitness.

It's expected that any idea worth sharing will be subject to scrutiny and debate. While my team and I work directly and successfully with businesses to establish workplace mental fitness in practice, we acknowledge that the term 'mental fitness' itself has never been precisely defined after it was first suggested in 1964 by developmental psychologist Dorothea McCarthy as 'a more appropriate term to describe the positive aspects of mental health'.

If we don't have a well-defined term, managers can't be expected to know exactly what it is and how they should be trained in it. Therefore, my company LinkPADD, in collaboration with Meeting for Minds, has also commissioned research at the University of Notre Dame to advance the understanding of mental fitness as a concept.

While anticipating the results of this research, this book will serve as a beacon to navigate the way to workplace mental fitness.

The concepts in **Part I: Setting the Scene** are distilled from over a decade of hands-on gritty management work. Deep in the trenches of real-world organisations, I observed, analysed, hypothesised, discussed, executed, reviewed and improved my management techniques in a continual cycle of progress.

I am excited that this book shares my methods for success with more people than I could personally meet. More importantly, it invites academic institutions to involve real-world organisations in their research on the leading edge of workplace mental health and fitness.

The seeds of each chapter in **Part II: Making It Real** come from the people and organisations my co-author John and I encounter in the course of our work. I would often be inspired after a client meeting, thinking, 'This is exactly what's happening in the real world! I must add it to the book!' John, an ace trainer who knows our system inside out, provides substantial explanatory content as well.

We would share these gems of thought with our co-author Alexis, who then adds her word alchemy. She turns our words into gold to make our ideas shine, and weaves in quite a few eloquent gems of her own.

There are new ideas in this book that some readers may find disturbing, insulting, or politically incorrect. If that's what it takes to jolt you out of your stupor, it's doing its job. If you are easily offended, please put this book down and get a golf magazine or something. However...

If you want to know how to create a workforce that's on fire, not burnt out, stick with us.

Let's build organisations where people love to work, where success loves to live, and where growth in many forms loves to thrive.

I look forward to providing thought leadership in this space to contribute something of value to education and training.

I leave you with the inspiring words of Rhonda Brighton-Hall, CEO of mwah. (making work absolutely human):

> Work is a core component of our existence, our identity, our financial independence, and, ultimately, our overall wellbeing. A happy workplace where people feel valued can increase productivity and innovation and reduce unwanted outcomes like employee absenteeism, workplace grievances and staff turnover.

'Link:Flow:Grow' is my mantra for manifesting happy workplaces. I welcome you to join us, and explore the possibilities with honesty and courage.

Kristopher G. Harold
Perth, Western Australia
January 2018

Introduction

The purpose of this book is to share a new and effective way to overcome critical workplace issues that have not gone away despite the best efforts of leaders and expert consultants.

We're talking about big challenges that affect revenue growth, productivity, profitability, employee engagement, staff turnover, quality, compliance, safety, performance culture and more.

If your organisation takes action on what this book recommends, you can start a new momentum that cascades results in three months, six months, 12 months. And you can apply this practical leadership guide to your own workplace straight away. All levels of management and staff can participate in creating a self-sustaining workplace with long-term business excellence.

As business expert Peter Drucker famously said, 'Management is doing things right; leadership is doing the right things.' So what are the 'right things' that we recommend, and will help you implement? Taking stock of where your organisation truly is right now (with brutal honesty), and laying a strong new foundation of high performance by developing workplace mental fitness.

We also resonate with Michael Abrashoff's view that 'When leaders explore deep within their thoughts and feelings in order to understand themselves, a transformation can take place.'[4]

This book is a resource for business owners, directors and managers (and useful reading for anyone who works with others, whether you play a white-collar or blue-collar role) to explore deep within. We invite you to look at old issues from fresh new perspectives. Think differently, then do things differently to get the results you want.

We are excited to introduce Link:Flow:Grow, a proven new paradigm for organisational design and development that builds a mentally fit workplace culture. Such an environment supports good mental health in individuals. Our results show that if we get the 'management' part of it right in-house by working on workplace mental fitness, you won't get as many issues that need the intervention of mental health professionals.

This book is divided into two main parts.

In **Part I: Setting the Scene**, we go over key ideas and concepts that have guided our work in the last decade or so. Senior leaders and managers can benefit by adding each concept to their management toolkit. At the end of each chapter, you are invited to apply the reading to your own situation with a Mental Fitness Stretch. Let the questions and suggestions spark insights, guide discussions and inspire actions. With these seeds for improvement, start changing what is in the way of your success.

In **Part II: Making It Real**, we share stories and anecdotes on how the concepts in part I work in real life. Our first book reviewers have found the stories highly relatable to their day-to-day experience.

Together with the stories, we provide a toolkit you can use right away. We understand your problems because we've lived through them as frontline managers. And these are the same tools we used to turn things around. Names, places and other details may have been changed to protect the guilty, but these are real situations that many recognise. With each chapter, we also share insights to encourage you to apply learnings more deeply.

Our writing style is intentionally light and colloquial, as we don't want it to be an academic textbook. (Grammar wise, we use the gender neutral 'their' or 'they' to avoid the clumsy 'his/her' or 'he/she' wording.) Some parts are meant to appeal to the analytical left brain, and some appeal to the intuitive and visual right brain. You don't need to agree with this classification to benefit from reading it; just know we hope we have succeeded in creating a whole-brain experience.

This book helps you understand why your best efforts may have not brought more success in the past. It helps you connect the dots between ten 'must-have' areas many managers think are 'nice-to-haves', so you can see with new eyes to ask better questions and discover better answers. Answers that help you achieve practical success as a high-performance workplace without burnout.

Keep the following questions in mind as we embark on a hero's quest from mayhem to workplace mental fitness with Link:Flow:Grow:

- **Link.** What critical links do you need to establish in your Intelligent Org Chart (IOC)? How do you use the IOC to address burnout? (You'll learn all about the IOC in chapter 5.)

- **Flow.** How do you shift from burnout to flow? Are you and your team members mentally fit and why does it matter?

- **Grow.** Where do your organisation (Company), your Team and your Self—CTS—want to be in six months, two years, five years, ten years? How do you create an environment that inspires and supports every individual to perform at their best?

You could read this book from start to finish, or pick and choose any chapter or story that takes your fancy. If you're a business owner or senior manager championing change, you may want to get a full picture of the Link:Flow:Grow system by reading the whole of part I, then dip into part II for the stories that interest you. These stories capture real people and situations we encountered while helping our clients turn their companies around, and some personal anecdotes. We'll share the change management tools we used in each case, and hopefully entertain you as well.

Every organisation, large or small, provides a wonderful environment for teaching and developing the practical benefits of workplace mental fitness. We must encourage managers to learn how to add value to everyone's mental wellbeing.

Let's begin!

PART I
Setting the Scene

In part I, we start by explaining why you cannot influence mental health without first taking care of workplace mental fitness, and how this is the answer to burnout management.

Then in chapter 3 you get a bird's-eye view of the Link:Flow:Grow system that outlines how to take care of workplace mental fitness as managers. (This means you are not expected to manage mental health, which is outside your area of expertise, and are instead taught what you can and should do as a manager to create a high-performing work environment with a strong foundation of workplace mental fitness.)

We go deeper into the Link aspect of our system. After satisfying the left-brainers with a mathematical equation for creating organisational brilliance, in chapter 5 we sink our teeth into the Intelligent Org Chart (IOC) and its 10 Bands of interrelated management functions. Here we explain why you need to get your ducks in a row in bands 1 to 9 as pillars for Band 10, where you establish an EveryBest workforce strong in workplace mental fitness (congratulations!).

As you achieve the goals of each band, you can give yourself a pat on the back for achieving excellence in that business area. If there are some who still cannot perform well, despite workplace support, these people may have deeper personal issues best handled by mental health professionals.

In the Link:Flow:Grow system, it is important to clarify the roles of the four types of leaders (which often get mixed up in real life). We do that in chapter 7, then discuss in chapter 8 what it takes to be a high-impact leader competent in HIL climbs.

We'll chat more in chapters 9 to 11 about the kind of leader you need to be (and should not be) to Link, Flow and Grow a winning culture and high-performing workforce. We like this bit a lot: to many of our clients it is a wake-up call and catalyst for tremendous growth as leaders.

And if you survive how uncomfortable those chapters make you feel, you are rewarded with utopia in chapter 12: EveryBest in action. This is what we are all aiming for—it's the 'Grow' part of our paradigm. Yes, it is possible to achieve this, and it is sustainable.

Chapter 1
Workplace mental fitness

Mental fitness is the essence that underpins the greatest achievements. You see it in a spectacular sporting feat or an artistic masterpiece. You hear it in the calm and kind response to a torrent of verbal abuse. You feel it when you're swept away by an epic piece of music. You recognise it in that truck driver who waves you to merge in peak-hour traffic with a smile. These are examples of individual mental fitness.

For the purpose of creating high-performing teams without burnout, we focus on collective workplace mental fitness, which is made up of the mental fitness of individuals in the organisation.

A person with high mental fitness is aware and assertive, resilient and respectful, considerate and collaborative. A person with low mental fitness can be accusatory or argumentative, distrustful or untrusting, competitive or careless.

An organisation made up of people with high individual mental fitness creates great workplace mental fitness that underpins a high-performance organisational culture without burnout.

You want to establish great workplace mental fitness as it is the bedrock, the lifeblood, the springboard and every other amazing metaphor propelling your organisation's stratospheric success.

Mental fitness and mental health

Mental fitness and mental health are two different concepts.

'Mental health' tends to be associated with negative traits such as depression, anxiety and paranoia, and has a stigma attached to it. It refers to the wellness of the individual's mind, in the realm of psychology.

'Mental fitness' is associated with positive mind states such as resilience, cheerfulness and adaptability, and has no attached stigma. Our interest is in workplace mental fitness—the wellness of the organisation's mindset or culture—in the realm of sociology.

When told they need to implement a mental *health* program at work, managers often can't relate to it as part of their job. They can't link it directly to company deliverables and regard it as a 'nice-to-have'. Even if they recognise the value of it, they don't have the skills of a mental health professional to really take care of their people's mental health.

A mental *fitness* program, on the other hand, is a management tool for taking care of the workforce. It is a 'must-have'. It's a manager's job to, well, *manage* their people to bring out their best. This gives the workforce the best chance to fulfil the goals of the organisation.

In our consulting work, we have demonstrated time and time again that it is the confusion of mental health with mental fitness that prevents organisations from getting the results they want. They don't get their desired results because they have not built up workplace mental fitness.

Here's an analogy. If you are physically fit, go to the gym regularly and play sports, it doesn't mean you can't have health issues. But research says you are giving yourself the best shot at staying physically healthy.

Same thing with mental fitness. If you are mentally fit and regularly practise mindfulness, it doesn't mean you don't or won't have a mental health issue such as depression. However, keeping mentally fit gives you the best possible chances of having fabulous mental health.

Workplace culture

If managers look after an organisation's culture, they create a workplace where individuals are empowered to look after themselves. Workplace culture can have a great impact on the mental health of employees.

So what is workplace culture?

It's the 'how we do things around here' that results from the 'what we think of our people, and what we need to do to succeed in our business' mentality of the leadership. Very often, in a place that puts profits before people, the workplace culture will suck, and guess what! Ironically, it affects profits in the long run.

As managers, we are responsible for the *mental fitness* of our workplace culture. This is part of our job to optimise business performance. In contrast, it is neither our job nor our expertise to focus on the *mental health* of individuals. Leave that to the psychologists and psychiatrists.

Whenever we say this to people, we get a variety of responses. They go 'Aahhh!' and a light bulb goes 'ding' and lights up in their minds. Or they go 'Ohhhhhhh ...' and heave a slow sigh of relief. Some go 'Huhh?', so let's clarify it for you.

Workplace mental fitness does not guarantee individual mental health. It can, however, influence individual mental health in a big way.

When an organisation is mentally fit, it provides the best environment for its individuals to be in great mental health. At one level, occupational burnout may seem to be about mental health: an overworked doctor commits suicide. An overworked project manager turns alcoholic. An overworked designer plunges into depression and develops an eating disorder. An overworked truck driver gets road rage and kicks a motorist, crashes a car, or throws things at another driver.

When you zoom in, you see mental health problems at the individual level. When you zoom out, we can guarantee you there are mental *fitness* problems at the organisational level. Many workplace mental health programs are impotent because they are barking up the wrong tree.

For every doctor, project manager, designer or truck driver who hits boiling point, there are thousands of others simmering under the surface, soldiering on, being slowly eroded by stress day after day. If we, as managers, don't do something to manage the heat and cool things down, there will be more eruptions, some of them fatal.

To prevent our workforce from experiencing such sorry states, the first thing to look at is their alertness.

Alertness first: MaxWell Mind

Workplace mental fitness is not hard to implement. The first thing you need is an alertness program. If your people have been suffering from burnout and fatigue, they won't be in the right state of mind to develop mental fitness.

To develop alertness, say hello to MaxWell Mind. He's a great imaginary friend we introduce at workshops. He reminds us to perform with a maximum wellness of mind and we encourage everyone to get acquainted with him.

In MaxWell's mind, fatigue is your friend. It is a signalling system from our perfectly engineered human bodies that we are not functioning at our optimum. Accepting our humanness means accepting that we will experience times of low alertness and high alertness. Allow individual differences in the work environment.

When we accept and allow human beings to be human beings, we can manage fatigue more effectively.

How do managers say 'I care about your fatigue' through their actions?

One way is to provide SmartCap[5] technology to site workers and truck drivers. It's a biofeedback device that monitors fatigue and eliminates microsleeps.

In a mentally unfit workplace, workers would be nervous about revealing so much of the inner workings of their minds; the data could be potentially damning. But in a mentally fit workplace, workers feel supported by this technology, as is intended by management.

Failure is not having poor SmartCap data. Failure is falling asleep and crashing into a tree.

Impact of alertness tracking

Malcolm, our safety adviser, didn't want to wear the SmartCap. He was on a two-on, one-off swing on a remote mine site. (If you're unfamiliar with fly-in fly-out work rosters, that means he flew in to the worksite and worked for two weeks, typically on 12-hour shifts, then flew out and had a week off.)

Before SmartCap, Malcolm, a 27-year-old, vaguely knew he had a sleep issue but never did anything about it. His data prompted him to seek medical help, and he discovered he had sleep apnea. Early discovery, early intervention. Imagine if we never found out what was affecting his productivity? The lifetime trajectory of his career performance could have been affected.

To create a high-performance workforce, managers need to commit to improving alertness. The rules can be simple: accept human fatigue, and design programs to maximise fitness for work.

MaxWell Mind recommends workplace mental fitness (WMF).

WTF is WMF?

In our books, not looking after something as important as the mental fitness of your workforce is inexcusable. Let us share a piece of our impassioned right brains before our 'civilised' left brain takes over in the next section.

So WTF is WMF and why should anyone care? Because it irritates us that there is a lot more talk than action taken to address mental wellbeing in most workplaces and we want to eliminate the airy-fairy BS.

It's all well and good for white-collar managers to spout abstract concepts and quote industry statistics. But if you don't translate that into something practical and meaningful, you will have no impact.

Mental fitness is not intangible. It is not unattainable. What you measure, you can improve.

A practical manager translates workplace mental fitness into concrete measurable data specific to the individuals and teams in their organisation. Besides tracking alertness, we have the DASS-21 diagnostic tool for depression, anxiety and stress; safety and workplace injury statistics; physical and mental duty-of-care records; and workers compensation figures.

Do you track this data at your workplace and relate it to organisational performance? Do your managers know the signs of depression, anxiety and stress, and are they ready to step in if required?

We challenge you to know your data and manage your workplace mental fitness appropriately. The journey of self-discovery in an environment of supported development can transform your people and workplaces. It already has for the companies that have embraced Link:Flow:Grow as a way of life at work.

Workplace mental fitness is built up from individual mental fitness. For example, my (Kris's) aim is to sustain my ability to perform at my peak in my role while still being a great father to my three kids. I need to be alert and have high energy levels for them on top of the 100 per cent I give at work. I monitor my high alertness and low alertness times during the day and ensure that I eat well and exercise. I must also be careful to taper periods of high stress with strategies to lower stress levels. I must actively disengage from the stress and mentally recuperate. I also need to be sure to step back and celebrate my successes, not just plough on through my week.

This is simple stuff. But many of us have lost our way and we need to take stock. The most powerful way to create workplace mental fitness is to start with yourself. There is no such thing as perfect but we can certainly be at the optimum. Be the change you want to see in your workplace. Create a business that understands WTF WMF is.

The mentally fit workplace

A mentally fit workplace reduces burnout, keeps stress manageable, increases work satisfaction and enhances business performance.

We all deserve better, and as a manager you can do something to make it happen.

The first thing to do is change the way you perceive mental fitness. Mental fitness is not a 'nice-to-have', it's a 'must-have'. When you hear these common myths that keep organisations stuck, challenge them:

- 'Mental fitness is about soft skills, we do that when we have time.'
- 'We don't train our managers to understand soft skills, they are just supervisors.'
- 'Soft skills are not important; we need to work.'
- 'Work is the most important part of my day.'
- 'Caring about feelings means you are not working.'

These are the people who don't know that we have known for 100 years that soft skills are vital to professional success. Research conducted by Harvard University, the Carnegie Foundation and Stanford Research Center have all concluded that **85 per cent of job success comes from having well-developed 'soft' and people skills**, and only 15 per cent of job success comes from technical skills and knowledge (or 'hard' skills).[6]

In a workplace where managers empower, support, mentor and acknowledge employees, there's high engagement and productivity. There are very clear correlations between mental fitness and business performance. You can tell which organisations get this: the clues are in their duty of care and workplace health and safety policies.

Mentally fit organisations have policies that demonstrate they value their people, provide ongoing mentoring, and regard them with trust and respect.

Done right, these policies create wellbeing and engagement across all levels of the organisation. Such success is possible when policies are not decreed by armchair generals disconnected from what their people are experiencing in the field.

Mental fitness can flow to all parts of an organisation when there is an action plan with clear links of accountability.

Here is a typical action plan:

Sample action plan

1. **Where are we now?**

   a. Start by understanding the problems and issues of the organisation.

   b. Where needed, conduct a root cause analysis to understand why things are the way they are.

   c. Map the current organisational chart, and review how each role (not the person, the role) is fulfilling organisational objectives ... or not.

All too often people are blamed for why things go wrong. When you dig deeper, you discover what really created the issues. We often find that important links and protocols are either not in place or not working. You can't build a great culture if the rotten bits aren't removed.

2. **Where do we want to be?**

   a. *Stop the bleeding.* Yup, some companies come to us having done the very best they could, but sales keep plummeting, great people keep leaving, or workers compensation claims keep rising. Often, we are in a situation where we need to turn a business around really fast. All hands are on deck but they lack a workplace mental fitness champion who can lead the organisation out of the storm.

   b. *Prevent further bleeding.* They can see it on the horizon—cashflow slowing down and threatening to go red; insurance premiums rising like a hot air balloon, threatening to make the business go 'pop'.

   c. *Increase high performance.* Unlike the first two scenarios (where we need to implement Link:Flow:Grow right away or go bust), this proactive scenario is to build on existing positive momentum and take a leap into a new stratosphere of success. Happily, the same companies in the first two scenarios often arrive at the third within 12 to 24 months of diligent organisational restructure.

3. **How do we get there?**

   a. A changing culture needs a champion who exercises their MBWA—Management by Walking Around. This leader walks the floor and challenges the status quo, and is someone with the engagement skills to connect with people to make things work.

(continued)

Sample action plan (*cont'd*)

b. Whoever is proposing the change needs to take charge of the journey and get to the end goal. In these cases, how things are done is as important as the outcomes you seek. When the journey develops collaboration, respect and understanding, you know that you have created an excellent foundation for ongoing success.

c. The organisation needs a cultural plan. Through it, everyone works together to create an environment where mental stressors are minimised, and a connected, resilient workforce continually improves to increase efficiencies, safety and wellbeing. Metaphorically, this is the sustainable way to fatten up your golden geese to produce more and more golden eggs sustainably.

d. Create an Intelligent Org Chart (IOC) of optimum roles without including employee names just yet. The restructured org chart becomes a guiding focus to update position descriptions, especially with the high-concept and high-touch skills that are missing.

e. Allocate people who fit the refreshed roles. To help each person succeed, fit the right personality to the role, and prepare them to deal with change and uncertainty—workplaces and roles do not stay static forever.

f. Communicate the updated game plan and expectations to the workforce. Consider using a best practice assessment tool to assess gaps and customise training and coaching (to enhance a person's ability to Think, Lead, Influence and Change).

g. For those who do not fit the updated roles, collaborate with managers to find alternate roles for staff if possible. If not possible consider managing out options (redundancy, etc.). This approach provides balance in treating people with respect while focusing on success goals.

Now you have a clearer human resource management plan for both existing employees and potential new hires.

4. How will we know when we're there?

a. Measure the 'Before' and 'After' effects of Link:Flow:Grow.

b. Measure and compare all major business performance and operational KPIs. But wait, there's more, and it's much better than free steak knives.

c. Observe daily behaviour at the workplace: what people are saying to themselves and each other, how they are interacting with each other, above and below their levels, and with customers, suppliers and other stakeholders. Encourage behaviour that builds workplace mental fitness, and counsel behaviour that erodes it.

5. What will we do to celebrate milestones?

a. This is just as important as all the work you get done in the previous stages of the action plan. It positively anchors your achievements in celebratory experiences, which can be big or small. Bonus points if you can activate team bonding as well.

b. Rest a while, then continue with the next iteration of organisational improvement. Start again from 'Where are we now?' and keep building your workplace mental fitness with continual improvement.

The Link:Flow:Grow action plan builds workplace mental fitness from strong foundations, and has achieved phenomenal results in a variety of organisations. It minimises the likelihood of burnout, stress, fatigue and other wellbeing issues that undermine a high-performance culture. It works because it was conceived by frontline managers who have lived the workplace challenges they are helping organisations to tackle. It stems from a deep understanding of why chaos reigned, and how to successfully turn things around.

Why did chaos reign in the first place? Because there were no other mechanisms to prevent or reverse it. When managers and employees use defensive blame games and excuses for not achieving targets, it feeds chaos.

How does workplace mental fitness counter chaos? Because where mental fitness resides there is flow. Flow does not feed on excuses or blame. Flow is about treating people with trust and respect, being competent in planning actions to drive results, and tapping into expertise with integrity.

Before we delve deeper into how Link:Flow:Grow gets us where we want to go, let's talk about burnout.

Mental Fitness Stretch

- What would it be like if there were far better ownership of the business at team level?

- Consider what it would be like to have more time to focus on the business and not the issues.

Chapter 2
Burnout

Organisations cannot afford to ignore workplace mental fitness if they want to minimise the crippling effects of burnout.

What is burnout?

Burnout is physical, emotional and mental exhaustion caused by the stress of being exposed to demanding work situations for a long time. It is a serious workplace health and safety issue, as untreated mental health conditions alone are estimated to cost Australian workplaces about $11 billion every year.[7]

According to Safe Work Australia, work-related stress has been linked with high levels of:

- unplanned absences, including sick leave
- staff turnover
- withdrawal and presenteeism
- poor work and poor product quality.[8]

Work-related stress may also lead to depression and anxiety in the long term, and workers with severe depression take 20 times more sick leave per month than the average worker.

Why do people get burnt out?

Burnout can originate from one or more of these external workplace factors:

- a poorly designed or managed work environment
- mentally, physically or emotionally demanding work
- excessive or prolonged work pressures
- bullying or harassment
- a traumatic event
- workplace violence.

On an individual level, internal factors that may contribute to burnout include:

- skills not being aligned with roles
- levels of tolerance or resilience not aligning with what they have to deliver at work
- poor habits related to sleep, exercise, water consumption and mobile phone use
- a tendency to put others' needs first and not prioritising self-care
- lack of social support
- lack of assertiveness, not being able to say no
- inability to manage emotional stress, self-soothe, or ask for help.

Burnout is very real, and it steals motivation, passion and endeavour often without the person knowing it. Mentally fit organisations don't let it happen.

What do mentally fit organisations do to prevent burnout?

They recognise that individual wellbeing is a key ingredient for the organisation's success, and systematically boost it:

- Their workplace mental fitness champion researches the signs and symptoms of fatigue, stress and anxiety, and puts together solutions to better control it.

- They look at job fit, rosters and resources.

- They seek feedback from everyone involved to find the likely causes of burnout.

- They redesign, restructure and reshape people and teams in a practicable way so that everyone benefits.

One guy's experience with burnout

Corporate high-flyer Sean Hall was inspired to research burnout after he caught himself wandering around a David Jones department store not knowing how he got there, on the verge of a complete nervous breakdown.[9] He had exceeded every goal in his senior executive role but didn't feel successful anymore.

He noticed that many companies are now in the habit of

> downsizing and downsizing until you are doing someone else's job as well as yours and feel as though you can't say no or admit you are struggling, for fear of damaging your reputation.

The 2017 mwah. report 'Happy workers: How satisfied are Australians at work?'[10] shows that almost a third of Australians are dissatisfied with their pay and working hours. It also reveals that 'higher education doesn't provide higher workplace happiness'.

Something major needs to change. People need to hear it's okay to not be perfect.

What are the warning signs of burnout?

Preventing burnout includes switching on your radar to look out for signs of it developing, in your employees or in yourself.

See figure 2.1 for an excellent diagnostic tool from the Australian Institute of Management to check if you are burnt out.

Figure 2.1: Are you burnt out?

CHANCES ARE YOU ARE SUFFERING FROM BURNOUT

Source: Australian Institute of Management.

These are also useful ways to look out for the warning signs of burnout in your work mates.

If you find yourself experiencing any of the symptoms above, please don't beat yourself up about it. Focus on making small positive changes, be kind to yourself, and be open to help and support.

How do we tackle burnout? Here's five great ways to start:

1. Drink lots of water.

2. Make mindful healthy food choices.

3. Get out into the fresh air.

4. Move in a way that brings you joy.

5. Chill and quieten your mind.

Pick one and do it right now. It takes only a few minutes, yet could disrupt your burnout's momentum to put you back on track.

Then, settle in and read the next chapter because that's where we introduce you to a practical and effective way to stop burnout and build a high-performance culture. It's called Link:Flow:Grow, and implementing it will transform your organisation by releasing the power of workplace mental fitness.

Mental Fitness Stretch

- Imagine workplace burnout transforming into high performance flowing from a more empowering and efficient way of working. What would it be like to experience a day in the life of this workplace? Be as vivid as you can!

- What beliefs may be contributing to burnout in your workplace? (E.g. the belief that only one person can be trusted to do a specific job.)

- How does poor job fit affect work-related stress?

- How well have previous audits identified these issues and their causes?

Chapter 3
Link:Flow: Grow

'Workplaces are stressful. That's just the way it is.'

Most people are resigned to this 'fact'. And if their workplace is demoralising, they often just bear with it and soldier on, because that, too, is expected of a workplace.

Happily: No. *No.* NO.

Link:Flow:Grow fixes this. It stops burnout and builds a high-performance culture.

These *means* goals are 'must-haves' and not 'nice-to-haves', because they have a direct impact on *end* goals—business KPIs that matter. Some spectacular results are listed in the preface, and here are more. Workplaces that have implemented Link:Flow:Grow have seen:

- 400 per cent increase in revenue
- reduction of workers compensation premiums to 1 per cent
- 90 per cent reduction in serious safety incidents to under two a year.

PwC reports that organisations can expect an average ROI of 2.3 for every dollar invested in creating a mentally healthy workplace.[11] Our clients have achieved an ROI of 10 and more.

Managers may find this perspective difficult to accept, but if a workplace is stressful and demoralising, it is a management problem. But this is not as bad as it sounds, because problems have solutions.

Most people don't know what to do with such problems, but we do: Link:Flow:Grow.

What is Link:Flow:Grow?

Link:Flow:Grow is a practical management toolkit for powerful organisational design and development—developed by two frontline managers experienced in high-risk blue- and white-collar industries such as the transport, construction, manufacturing and mining industries.

Why is it such a great solution?

- It fills the missing link that has escaped other well-meaning approaches to workplace change management. Too many people in business try to achieve Growth and Flow before completing the fundamentals of Link.

- It has been developed by frontline managers for frontline managers, not by consultants spruiking lofty theories. We have lived through workplace problems similar to the ones our customers face.

- It empowers your organisation, as it is implemented by your people using your technology and systems. We merely help you get things started.

How does Link:Flow:Grow work? See figure 3.1.

Figure 3.1: Link:Flow:Grow helps organisations hit the bull's eye of human performance optimum

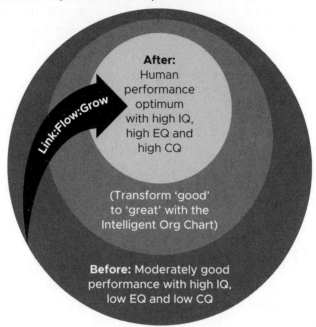

After:
Human performance optimum with high IQ, high EQ and high CQ

(Transform 'good' to 'great' with the Intelligent Org Chart)

Before: Moderately good performance with high IQ, low EQ and low CQ

Link:Flow:Grow takes a right-brain IQ-driven workplace and makes it great. It introduces EQ-centric values using the Intelligent Org Chart (IOC), and augments it with CQ (Collaborative Quotient). This creates a mentally fit workplace that operates at its EveryBest and achieves human performance optimum. This is a high-performance workforce without burnout. Don't worry, all these concepts will be explained in the chapters to come!

Why does Link:Flow:Grow matter?

According to Safe Work Australia, which has tracked work-related traumatic injury fatalities since 2003, transport and construction have consistently ranked in the top three[12] industries for worker fatalities, with manufacturing and mining in the sixth and seventh spots respectively for 2016.

While their 2016 report announces the lowest fatality rate in 14 years, having an average figure of 20 workers dying per month is still 20 too many. It is also worrisome that 92 per cent of workers affected by workplace trauma and fatalities are men.

The physical, emotional and mental components of workplace burnout are often entangled.

Some workplaces seem to drift from one disaster to another, and nothing seems to flow. Everyone has an issue or their own agenda to run that is not aligned with the company's agenda, and this creates so many problems for the effective flow of work.

Link:Flow:Grow provides a systematic way to address this, to maximise organisational engagement and build an excellent workplace culture.

What does Link:Flow:Grow do?

Let's look at the key components of this system to better understand how we get these processes to work together. We'll illustrate these steps with examples from a transport company we've worked with.

Link structured resources

'Link' refers to the linkage of effective systems, competent people and efficient use of resources. This is a critical first step to ensure that people, equipment and environment all harmonise. This takes effort and vision, and you had a taste of what is involved in the action plan in chapter 1.

Most seniors in an organisation may see the bigger picture but may not stop to survey the collective activity and synergies required from each team or work group, and link them with systems and resources to improve operations. Once these are linked, there can be flow.

Case study: Transport company (Link)

John investigated a transport company where their fleet of trucks repeatedly delivered the wrong products to the wrong customers, threatening future business. In this case, the links of accountability were broken, so no productivity or quality flowed.

Poor recruitment practices fed high staff turnover and low operational discipline, so no wonder nobody knew what they were doing.

Their workplace mental fitness champion conducted an investigation and found that there were neither linkages between work groups nor one system to manage the big picture. The champion established a coherent system, instilled the value that if they helped each other they would all get it right, and implemented pre-start engagement meetings to build accountability.

Flow mental fitness

In operational terms, 'flow' refers to increasing throughput while upholding quality and customer satisfaction. The concept originates from positive psychology, as the mental state of energised and immersive focus and enjoyment of a task.

It is absolutely possible for managers to create a work environment where operations are carried out productively while people are in a high-performance state. That's what great managers do, instead of pointing fingers at specific people for stuffing up.

Flow is a consequence of Link. When good people, systems and protocols are in place, they synergise and help each other to move forward. So, to get flow you need to undertake the IOC audit in chapter 5 and carefully consider your game plan. The more effort you put into building the mental fitness of your people, systems and processes, the easier flow will happen.

Case study: Transport company (Flow)

With the right links in place, there is a smooth flow of supervision and communication even when people and resources are transferred from team to team, and everyone works harmoniously to achieve a common goal. As flow increases, people are for more satisfied at work, and customer complaints are now scarce.

Grow workplace success

Once flow abounds, success naturally grows, either as processes for continual improvement, or as part of the business plan, fuelled by people who are competent and motivated to succeed.

Grow results from Link and Flow. Where mental fitness abounds, ideas for continual improvements just seem to manifest spontaneously in every part of the organisation. It is amazing what you can do with the time not occupied by fighting fires, resolving conflicts and doing re-work. Get rid of these stressful and demoralising experiences, and see what you naturally get as a result. The high-performance workforce can now make more happen with less, respond positively to challenges, and create new methods and possibilities with endless ideas.

Case study: Transport company (Grow)

The company establishes a great reputation for reliability and efficiency as a result of what was implemented by the workplace mental fitness champion, and secures new contracts now that they effectively provide more value to customers.

Why flow is important

To be alive and vibrant, there must be flow.

Without flow, there's stagnation, lack of growth, decay, and death.

This is true for both the blood in your veins and the lifeblood of your business.

Flow is a critical part of the Link:Flow:Grow process. It's a natural *consequence* of mentally fit linkages, and the natural *cause* of business growth.

To be 'in the flow' is to be fully immersed in an activity for its own sake, with energised focus and complete absorption. Also known as being 'in the zone', 'flow' was popularised in the Western world by Mihaly Csikszentmihalyi, a founding father of positive psychology.[13] The concept has existed for thousands of years under other guises, notably eastern religions. Inspired by his own experiences and Carl Jung, Csikszentmihalyi brought flow into the realm of psychology.

Today, it is used in a variety of fields and has an especially big recognition in occupational therapy. There's also some exciting research being done on flow at the University of Notre Dame and Murdoch University, addressing real-world problems such as work stress and burnout.

Flow is the *opposite* of burnout.

Training people to experience flow at work helps them to be more efficient and productive.

Now, here's an important distinction: flow is not dependent on reducing work hours or workloads.

Link:Flow:Grow is a practical solution. Reducing work is not a criteria for achieving flow. Making people work less is not a primary goal.

The goals are to achieve EveryBest, by developing workplace mental fitness.

Reducing burnout means helping workers to handle existing realities better. Lead them well, provide support, encourage skills development and enable them with the tools for building mental fitness (there are lots of these in part II).

Creating the state of flow

How do you, as a leader, create a state of flow in your workforce?

Start by asking yourself the Mental Fitness Stretch questions at the end of this chapter.

To paraphrase a popular quote attributed to Albert Einstein, it would be insane to expect a different result if you continued to do the same thing over and over again.

To create change, welcome the opportunity to be part of that change.

By developing high-concept, high-touch leaders in your workplace and being one yourself, you create the flow that will be the lifeblood of sustainable business success, no matter how challenging the environment.

In the next chapter, we shed more light on how you can accomplish this and more.

Mental Fitness Stretch

- Consider a workplace without streamlined processes and identify the range of issues this creates.

- Stand back and see if you can see the flow at work; if not, what do you see? Where are the blocks?

- What could you do to encourage more growth in the team?

- Consider what you might do with the time you save when Link:Flow:Grow is in place.

- What does it take to get mental fitness to flow through the entire workforce?

- Does the flow hit bottlenecks, preventing it from reaching your entire org chart? Where and what are these bottlenecks?

- What should be done to make sure management know how to enable the flow of mental fitness?

Chapter 4
Shining beyond brightness

In the arid red heart of Australia, out in the desert around Alice Springs, you'd think it would be pitch dark when the sun goes down.

But no.

Within sight of majestic Uluru, you can experience the enchanting Field of Light art installation by renowned British artist Bruce Munro. A luminous network of 50 000 glowing spheres floating on slender dendritic stems, blanketing an area the size of seven football fields.

Light is a common metaphor for success and all things good, so let's start here.

A shiny, happy organisation is a successful one. It's energised by lots of sunshine, everything is glowing and growing, the culture is thriving and positive, and you get lots of bouquets (i.e. compliments and appreciation).

If your workplace is full of problems, it can be a dark, gloomy place, laced with lethargy and stagnation. Nothing grows there. People don't see things very well, and it's hard for them to connect. They fumble in the dark, and have no idea what's going on around them.

Understandably, every organisation has light and shade. Here's why we are using this metaphor: how brightly your organisation shines is not solely based on how bright your people are.

The IQ/EQ/CQ formula for high workplace performance

It's not enough to have bright people (IQ) with impressive academic qualifications. In fact, some of these high achievers can be so intense they stress others out by shining their high beam right into their team members' eyes. Or they overshadow others in the organisation for personal glory.

Organisational brilliance is created by bright people (IQ) with high emotional intelligence (EQ) working well together collaboratively (CQ). It takes a combination of traditional smarts, a high emotional quotient, and a high collaborative quotient.

$$\text{Brilliance} = IQ \times EQ \times CQ$$

This is the formula for how brightly your organisation can shine.

It all starts with the quality of your people. Where it ends up depends on whether your organisation's state of mental fitness enhances or diminishes the brightness of your people.

An organisation's state of mental fitness can be observed as its culture when you walk into their office. It's not in the fittings. It's in the people.

Does the culture allow their people to shine brightly and illuminate others in their teams? Does it encourage letting someone else shine? Or does it hang a dark cloud over everyone's intrinsic light and reduce their luminance?

Case study: Bob the manager

Let us tell you how Bob, a senior manager, became a beacon in his gloomy workplace after John wired him up correctly and switched on his true capacity for brilliance.

In the 'Before' scenario, Bob went to work daily with the proverbial storm cloud over his head.

He was initially promoted to a senior managerial position without any demonstrated competence for that level. Not to say he didn't work hard. In fact, his home life was suffering because he donated endless hours fighting fires, coming up with excuses for failure and managing his time at work poorly.

He was so busy he could not do anything to stop the rising number of safety incidents and equipment damage happening in his patch. All incident investigations did for Bob was increase the pressure cooker that was his daily life.

His managers saw him crying for help and enrolled him in a leadership program. But guess what: he didn't even have the time to complete his assessment tasks and read the textbooks.

That was before he became a workplace mental fitness champion.

With the right coaching and support, Bob built up his mental fitness muscles and started to conquer chaos at work:

- He made considerable changes to the workplace environment under his control and reduced safety incidents and equipment damage counts.

- He spoke personally to each key member of his team and set higher performance expectations.

- Delegation freed up hours he could use to prioritise his day better and gain better work–life balance.

- As Bob shone brighter, his managers became more confident in his abilities and relaxed their micromanagement of him.

- As he developed maturity, wisdom and assertiveness, he started to mentor these traits by example into the supervisors working under him.

Bob's increase in IQ, EQ and CQ infected others, and they collectively increased organisational brilliance in the workforce. The old entrenched culture is not completely gone, and on some days Bob thinks he is going backwards. But he is really a 'two steps forward, one step back' kind of guy. He continues to make great inroads dispelling the darkness of chaos, and is pushing for succession planning.

The organisation can only shine brighter by continuing to adopt a humane approach that treats everyone with trust and respect to deliver success. Allow your people to shine, and your organisation will be brilliant.

Even if you're faced with a mental fitness desert in your workplace right now that has plunged it into darkness, you can install your own 'field of light' to connect and illuminate the whole organisation.

You can switch on the proverbial light bulb by using Link:Flow:Grow and the IOC to get to 'Oh! I see!'

Turn the page to start learning about the centrepiece of the Link:Flow:Grow process: the IOC.

Mental Fitness Stretch

- Would you say your work environment is light and bright, or dull and gloomy?

- How can you achieve the right balance of IQ and EQ?

- How would you rate the IQ, EQ and CQ of individuals in your workforce, and what impact have they on collective organisational brilliance?

Chapter 5

The Intelligent Org Chart (IOC)

The IOC is a powerful tool for building workplace mental fitness. It gives you your 'Oh! I see!' and tells you all the secrets of the organisation. The IOC is our primary framework for measuring and developing workplace mental fitness. Workplace mental fitness is what high-impact leaders put in place to create a high-performance culture. If you think of mental fitness as a spectrum from low to high, the highest rating of mental fitness expressing peak performance will be EveryBest, which we get into later in this chapter.

What is the IOC?

The IOC is a snapshot of the vitals of your organisation. It is the audit tool to be clear and focused on the pathway to success.

The IOC is a live organisational chart that provides a detailed picture of how well each role is hitting business targets. It links reporting and accountability relationships and the 'health scores' of ten performance bands (we go into the 10 Bands of the IOC in chapter 6).

The IOC provides a system for implementing High-Impact Leadership (HIL) in all areas of an organisation. HIL is achieved when managers are trained to facilitate Link:Flow:Grow.

By linking mentally fit roles and processes to create an IOC unique to your organisation, high-impact leaders facilitate the flow of workplace mental fitness that nourishes the growth of a high-performance workforce without burnout.

If you think you don't need an IOC, throw this book in the bin now.

Why is the IOC important?

If you take away only one thing from this book, we'd like it to be this: the IOC is the foundation for creating flow in your organisation.

Our frontline work has proven that the IOC creates real change by:

- identifying business-critical challenges
- outlining a sound change strategy to address them
- providing a practical framework to resolve these challenges.

The IOC is the bedrock of your organisation's stability and success.

Not just any org chart

'How intelligent is your organisational chart?'

'Huh?'

An organisational chart is an organisational chart, right? Isn't the intelligence in the organisation supposed to be in its people, not in the map of how the people are organised?

That manager went on to spout management speak at me (Kris), expounding scholarly concepts that sieved right through my young brain. The only thing that stuck was the term 'Intelligent Org Chart'.

I was a junior manager in the early 2000s and thrown into a role looking after the state of WA. I had limitless belief in my management capacity and was adamant that my truck drivers and yard staff were doing a great job.

I had great individuals but that hadn't translated into a cohesive high-performing team, and that annoyed and intrigued me in equal measure.

Their results were good—sometimes great—but never stable. At the time, I could not figure out why.

Fast forward to today.

Now I ask every business how intelligent their org chart is, and they look at me like I must have looked at my manager back then. I am always amazed at how little attention the org chart gets. When I ask to see it, the manager often pulls it out from a drawer or file and tells me it needs to be updated. Too often, structures are out of date and key issues have not been addressed.

I ask, 'What are the top priorities of the organisation this year and how does your org chart achieve them?'

I can almost see a giant black question mark loom over their heads as their puzzled eyes express their struggle to make sense of what I mean. 'Who's this guy? What are his management qualifications again?' their uncomfortable body language seems to say.

They may not warm up to me yet, but they keep listening.

I then ask, 'How is each position related to others and what is the flow of accountability?'

They go, 'Errmm, well, these are the job descriptions and these people report to those people like so ...'

Next, I ask, 'Look at this role, for example. Can you tell how well he is fulfilling his job description and what that contributes to [an important organisational objective]?'

At this point, their face is either starting to twitch or they are starting to bite their metaphorical fingernails. 'Errrm ... the org chart is not supposed to do that?'

The genius of the IOC

An Intelligent Org Chart will create a successful business environment if you:

- design it based on the roles needed to achieve your desired business outcomes — there should be **no names** in your org chart as we must focus on the function, not the person

- assess each **position profile** for function, not who you know

- have a leader and champion for a high-performance workplace culture — someone who builds engagement and assesses their skills gaps so you know exactly how to make them great

- review the IOC monthly and periodically, strip it back and **ask the hard questions** — is it functioning as it should? If not, why not?

- ensure your managers use **Key Result Areas** and **Key Performance Indicators**.

On top of KRAs and KPIs that every manager is taught to review, we add mental fitness strategies for increasing productivity, reducing staff turnover, improving safety and engagement, and reducing any workers comp failures.

Your IOC tells your Link:Flow:Grow story

We thoroughly enjoy unpacking the story that the org chart tells. Like any good story, it starts with key characters facing challenging scenarios (you meet a few of them in part II).

As it unfolds there will be opportunities and setbacks. Plot twists and progress. Gritty drama and conflict. Hopefully humour and epiphanies.

In the Link:Flow:Grow story, the hero enables more people to become heroes. The hero saves the day by first saving themselves. Together the workforce creates a culture where everyone succeeds: the Company, the Team and the Self (CTS). Individuals are mentored to lead themselves. The purpose of such leadership-focused organisational redesign is to achieve 'EveryBest'. This is the zone where organisations can truly overcome blocks and smash through brick walls. The Flow distributes workplace mental fitness across all parts of the organisation to Grow a high-performance culture where trust and respect create sustainable success.

In the next chapter, we show you the process for achieving this, by taking your business from Link to Flow using the IOC. We look at the 10 Bands of the IOC and how you need a degree of success with bands 1 to 9 before even starting to work on creating EveryBest, the Band 10 ideal.

Mental Fitness Stretch

- Consider the top priorities of your organisation this year. How does your org chart achieve them?

- If you are having systemic issues with performance failures or high incident rates, where are you capturing what each individual needs to do to overcome this?

- How is each position related to the others and what is the flow of accountability?

- Pick a person in any role in the IOC. Can you tell how well they are fulfilling their job description and how that contributes to any chosen important organisational objective?

Chapter 6

Rock the bands of the IOC

There are ten things you must get right before even thinking of tackling mental health issues or peak performance in the workplace. We call them the 10 Bands of the IOC.

Bands 1 to 9 are business areas that support the development of Band 10, an environment with strong workplace mental fitness that we call EveryBest (our business nirvana). When Band 10 is established, you have a great workplace environment that supports optimal mental health in individuals.

Why the 10 Bands matter

Too many organisations fail when they attempt to achieve a high-performance culture or stem burnout—because they haven't yet put their house in order in the business areas of bands 1 to 9. When bands 1 to 9 are in order, you achieve Band 10.

Until now, no-one has articulated an organisation design and development toolkit that understands the relationships among these business areas and how linking them creates transformation and stratospheric success.

When evaluating or managing large groups of workers to build a sustainable high-performance workplace culture, we see again and again that without a linked strategy for the 10 Bands:

- there is no High-Impact Leadership (HIL)
- workplace mental fitness cannot grow
- we can't create an environment that nurtures great mental health in individuals
- there is no foundation for the workforce resilience required to sustain that culture.

An IOC audit of the business areas covered in bands 1 to 9 reveals the fundamental issues in the organisation compared to benchmarked high-performing companies, and which of the bands need work and to what degree.

What are the 10 Bands of the IOC?

Let's unpack the 10 Bands of the IOC, the foundation of successful organisational redesign:

1. Key Deliverable Design
2. Org Design
3. Job Design
4. Managing 'In' Design (recruitment)
5. Induction Design
6. Training Design
7. Performance Development Design
8. Change Management Design
9. Managing 'Out' Design (exiting)
10. EveryBest Design (mental fitness first).

These 10 Bands are mapped in the Intelligent Org Chart as shown in figure 6.1.

Figure 6.1: The IOC

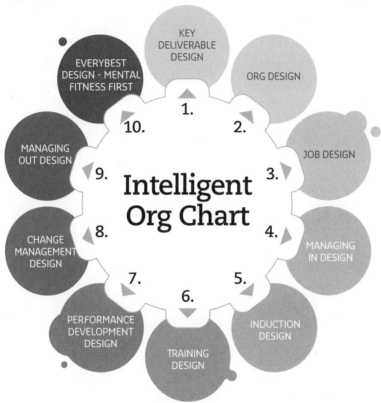

We need to get bands 1 to 9 functioning at 80 per cent or more before even starting to work on Band 10.

How to become a rock star at smashin' the 10 Bands

The following pages contain an introduction to the 10 Bands representing the key business functions that are essential for building a high-performance culture. For each band, we talk about:

- its key activity
- why it's important
- how to achieve it
- how it builds workplace mental fitness.

We also introduce the Visionary, the Driver, the Manager and the Frontliner: the four types of managers you need to create a high-performance culture. More on them in chapter 7.

Now let's look at each of the 10 Bands in more detail.

Band 1
Key Deliverable Design

Key activity
The Visionary mandates desired business outcomes.

Why it's important
You must know what you are aiming for before you can work towards achieving it.

How to achieve it
The Driver translates key deliverables into initiatives and plans in collaboration with Managers, who execute them via Frontliners.

How it builds workplace mental fitness
This is where the business decides mental fitness is a priority. Visionaries are pretty good at deciding this conceptually but practical support needs to be clear and focused.

Band 2
Org Design

Key activity
The Driver reviews the current org chart and redesigns it on principles of workplace mental fitness.

Why it's important
You need the right map to be successful in navigating the territory.

How to achieve it
Rock the IOC — see this chapter.

How it builds workplace mental fitness
The links of the organisation are a clear representation of the mental fitness of the workplace.
Org structures need to support optimum productivity and engagement.

Band 3
Job Design

Key activity

The Driver ensures that job descriptions contain both technical qualifications and character traits (e.g. high concept, high touch), and the right person is put into each role.

Why it's important

This will maximise productivity and minimise burnout to build a mentally fit high-performance team.

How to achieve it

Communicate job requirements, review performance regularly, support people to fulfil their roles well.

How it builds workplace mental fitness

All members of the workplace need to know their roles and how to be successful. Roles need to be clear and everyone needs to be set up for success.

Band 4
Managing 'In' Design

Key activity

The Driver hires and develops the right people for the roles.

Why it's important

The calibre and fit of your people determine the quality of results.

How to achieve it

Hire proven talent, establish succession plans and internships.

How it builds workplace mental fitness

When bringing someone into an organisation, it is critical to ensure the 'correct fit' for what the organisation is trying to achieve. The wrong hire can affect the mental fitness of the entire organisation.

Band 5
Induction Design

Key activity
The Driver ensures people are informed and supported to work safely at their best.

Why it's important
Your people are the geese who lay golden eggs for your organisation, not meat robots.

How to achieve it
Establish protocols and programs to uphold workplace wellbeing, enhance performance and manage stress.

How it builds workplace mental fitness
When you have the right person, you need to get them started with the best process. A good induction experience focused on key information and mentally fit practices makes a huge difference. Make sure every new starter knows that mental fitness matters!

Band 6
Training Design

Key activity

The Driver identifies what is needed to close skills gaps and ensures effective upskilling.

Why it's important

Workplace incompetence is a management issue if inadequate training is provided. If you can't change the people, change the people—if people can't be trained then they need to be managed out.

How to achieve it

Build a critical skills register for each role, know the difference between 'must-haves' and 'nice-to-haves', and be mindful of future skills requirements.

How it builds workplace mental fitness

Everyone has skills gaps and requires a development plan. Plans can be customised and don't have to cost a lot of money. The Link:Flow:Grow motto is 'Failure is not an option, only training'.

Band 7
Performance Development Design

Key activity
Ongoing high-touch performance management and role support by the Driver, Managers and Frontliners.

Why it's important
It minimises the disengagement and distress that lead to mistakes and incidents.

How to achieve it
Authentic influence that rewards success and counsels failure, and does not force people to comply based on your position of power, will achieve this.

How it builds workplace mental fitness
Effective performance management is a key component of employee success. All employees must know their KPIs and how they are essential for the organisation's future.

Band 8
Change Management Design

Key activity
All leaders work together to overcome the natural resistance to change, and transform people and processes to achieve continual improvement.

Why it's important
Stagnation reduces effectiveness and efficiency, and could threaten the enterprise's very existence.

How to achieve it
Analyse root causes of resistance and use a proven framework such as John Kotter's eight-step change model[14] to make it happen.

How it builds workplace mental fitness
Change is part of everyday work. When done right, it enhances workplace mental fitness. Employees are robust and disciplined when they are involved in creating change and genuinely engaged.

Band 9
Managing 'Out' Design

Key activity
Managing workforce redundancies and exits with a dignified and legally compliant protocol.

Why it's important
It benefits both the people who leave and those remaining in the workforce.

How to achieve it
Create a mentally fit exit protocol, and involve reputable professional agencies.

How it builds workplace mental fitness
When someone leaves, it doesn't need to be negative. Effective managing 'out' is a true skill and shows how much integrity and people management skills the leaders truly possesses. If you treat people wrong, it can destroy all your good work.

Band 10
EveryBest Design
(Mental Fitness First)

Key activity

Put mental fitness first: distribute power and accountability to all managers and leaders throughout your business and entrust them to be in control.

Why it's important

It builds a high-performance workforce that does not need to be micromanaged, and solid foundations for organisational flow.

How to achieve it

Achieve at least 80 per cent of KPIs and KRAs in bands 1 to 9.

How it builds workplace mental fitness

There are so many wonderful initiatives and programs to put into Band 10. A commitment by management to support effective synergies leads to true workplace mental fitness. The first program we suggest for any workplace is an Alertness Program (see chapter 1).

How the 10 Bands achieve flow

Most workplaces know and do some of the things in bands 1 to 9.

Badly. In silos.

They need to 'connect the dots' to operate a coherent system that tracks it all. With meticulous accountability where you know exactly how each person is doing their job while fulfilling overarching organisational objectives—or not.

Then you'll get flow. Not bottlenecks. Not stagnation. Not frustration.

Not overwhelm and burnout.

Quick case study: Workplace culture at a school

A school consulted us to stop the downward spiralling of workplace performance and accountability.

They aspired to create a workplace culture that:

- nurtures the wellbeing of individuals
- sets standards that the whole organisation can follow
- identifies with the future state of the business.

The IOC audit showed a lack of High-Impact Leadership (HIL) and a weak Band 4—Managing 'In' Design. Fixing that one element was already a great leap forward.

The school didn't have a scientific recruitment methodology, and only relied on what resumes said. We sat with them as they interviewed candidates for a new managerial role, easily spotted a high-impact leader, and recommended that hire.

The outcomes of the IOC audit were turned into targets and KPIs for all staff and tracked in their IOC management software.

Every workplace tells a different story in bands 1 to 9. In part II, we show some of the ones we've helped to rewrite into sensational bestsellers. Some of these real-life stories may even trigger a, 'Hey that's me!' response. Good! Then you know we can really help you.

In the next chapter we meet the people who make the bands rock and find out how they do it.

Failure along the way

EveryBest is not about never failing. It deals with the real world. It accepts that there are both positive outcomes (Success bucket) and negative outcomes (Failure bucket), as shown in figure 6.2.

Figure 6.2: Don't stay in the failure bucket

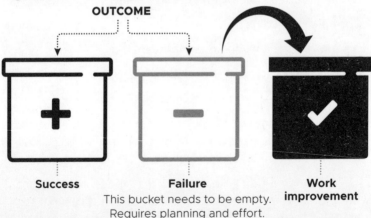

Success

Failure
This bucket needs to be empty.
Requires planning and effort.

Work improvement

Failure is not *in* the way of success, but *on* the way to success. It chalks up experience points. It is especially valuable when the person, team or company is venturing into new innovative territory. A high-performance team is not afraid of being punished for failure. But the team needs to be kicked in the butt if they do nothing about failure after it occurs.

Negative outcomes must be moved from the Failure bucket to the Work Improvement bucket as soon as possible.

A positive and diligent attitude to failure is vital to workplace mental fitness. Much more useful than a blame culture. And more enjoyable and fruitful for growth.

Mental fitness is about paying attention to a failure without blame or corporate tantrums, and moving the negative outcome into the Work Improvement bucket as soon as possible. Yes, senior managers, we're talking about you. Earning a higher salary does not give you the right to lose your temper at others.

Alertness comes first

Alertness is vital for preventing failure and reducing the impact when it does occur, harvesting failure's lessons for future success. That's why we recommend it as the first program to put in place to create workplace mental fitness. It doesn't need to be complicated.

First, ferret out the enemies of alertness: fatigue, stress and burnout. And do something about them.

Mental Fitness Stretch

- With your organisation in mind, rate how well it's rocking each band.

- What areas could be improved and what next step could you take?

- Consider how well the 10 Bands are connected in your management strategy.

Chapter 7

Who makes things happen?

It's not a pipe dream.

When we **Link** the right resources and processes based on our breakthrough system, the **Flow** of workplace mental fitness creates a high-performance culture that allows the Company, Team and Self to **Grow**.

This takes considerable design, planning, implementation and ongoing improvement.

But the resulting success will be worth the trouble, you'll see. But before getting to 'where we want to be', let's take a closer look at 'where we are now'.

A common scenario when things go wrong

When a workplace failure of any sort occurs, it is much too common for the proverbial carpenter (manager) to blame their tools (workers): Tom was lazy and incompetent, Dick had mental health issues, Harry was a greedy fraudster.

There is a tendency to point fingers at those closest to the failure incident. A dramatic example of this erupted on social media recently when the transport minister of a progressive country made a public statement that the maintenance team of a national transport company 'had failed us' when the 'preventable' flooding of an underground train tunnel affected hundreds of thousands of commuters.

The chairman and CEO of the company both apologised to the public. The chairman even bowed to show his deep regret. Of course, there were operational reviews and follow-up actions, which restored order within 20 hours (great result!). However, 'taking responsibility for the failure' also took punitive form. The senior executive in charge of maintenance got replaced. And team members were warned that their bonuses could be affected.

Punishment may be a common response to failure, but have you asked yourself if it is the best move (for both the short and long term) for creating a high-performance team? Mentally fit managers always consider long-term impact.

Consider that it is as useless to blame the maintenance team as it is to blame the CEO, chairman or minister for not doing their job.

If we assume that everyone is doing the best they can with what they know, might not the most useful thing be to focus on what could help everyone to do better, both bosses and workers?

Mentally fit carpenters don't blame their tools. **Mentally fit leaders don't blame and punish their staff.** Guided by mentally fit leaders, the very people involved in what went wrong can become the best people to make things right.

These leaders won't see their people as 'in the way', but 'on the way' to achieving better outcomes. They know how to mine failure for success. We turned exactly this situation around in three months when we overhauled the blame culture at a mechanical workshop. Oh, how satisfying it was to train the management to shift from blame and negativity to focus and united success!

You too can create mentally fit leaders who provide long-term big-picture solutions as well as immediate incident-specific ones to deal positively with failure.

How? Stick around, and meet our secret weapons. The people who bring the IOC to life and open the floodgates of high performance know how to link the 10 Bands of the IOC to create flow, and they play four leadership roles.

The four leadership roles

This section outlines the four types of mentally fit leaders who need to be planted in four levels of the organisation. Let's start with some general notes relevant to all four roles:

- The definitions and functional differentiators are simple in theory, yet often mixed up in practice. In real life, people tend to mix them up or take on more than one role. Want to know why this common practice is a recipe for disaster? Read on.

- The right-brain/left-brain distinction is used in a conceptual sense; it doesn't matter if you agree or disagree with its physiological reality.

- It's often that 'what you want' becomes clearer when you know 'what you don't want'. We've included notes of what the leader in each role shouldn't be, and are not surprised to have received feedback that this is often painfully relatable.

- Self-leadership is a powerful prerequisite for leading others. People who continually strengthen or upgrade themselves are more likely to possess the mind, heart and resilience to create workplace mental fitness that fuels a high-performance workforce. In fact, taking ownership empowers them to be phenomenally trusted and respected agents for change.

Although the breakthrough groundwork was done in the transport, construction, manufacturing and mining industries, the structure applies to any industry, with or without both blue-collar and white-collar workers.

Table 7.1: Four leadership roles that create EveryBest

The Visionary	• active right-brain skills • future-focused • sets the direction, expectations and key deliverables • provides the structure and resources to grow organisations • effective self-leader
The Driver	• active right-brain skills to augment left-brain prowess • future-focused, experienced senior business leader • assertive strategist • sets standards, delivers results • exercises 'high-concept' and 'high-touch' leadership skills • effective self-leader
The Manager	• left-brain active • present-focused • leader of large teams and work groups • focused on empowering Frontliners and helping them succeed • effective self-leader
The Frontliner	• left-brain active • present-focused • frontline supervisor of small teams • executes day-to-day • operational plans and tasks • effective self-leader

Now let's discuss these four roles in more detail.

The Visionary

This leader is the future-focused owner, director or other governance body who sets the direction, expectations and key deliverables for the next level of leader (the Driver), and provides the structure and resources to grow organisations.

Being right-brained doesn't mean they don't use their left brain, but that they exercise both IQ and EQ to innovate, strategise, make decisions, and interact with people. Speaking the language of the Herrmann Whole Brain Model, Visionaries use their intellect, intuition and instinct to focus on right-brained experimental and relational thinking, instead of rational left-brained analytical and practical tasks.

The best Visionaries find great Drivers, share their vision, then let go and trust them to do the job.

Some Visionaries need a wake-up call not to be dimwits. Dimwitted Visionaries cause the most damage, so it's better to be aware if you are one. The most spectacular dimwits are those who have no clue they are doing stupid and silly things — that sabotage the success of their company, teams, and people as individuals.

It is very possible for Visionaries to undo all the workplace mental fitness built over months and years if they do something stupid — usually a knee-jerk shadow of an old habit.

To Visionaries with companies in dire straits: you cannot just hire someone to make the problem go away without rolling up your French-cuffed sleeves to help. Be open to the possibility that you are part of the problem. Be brave. You can emerge a star, and save your company as well. It's cathartic, you'll see.

The Driver

Drivers are future-focused, experienced leaders who strategise, set standards and deliver results while exercising 'high-concept' and 'high-touch' leadership skills — which are primarily right-brain processes. We explore 'high concept, high touch' further in chapter 8.

The Driver is the catalyst for transformation. They have the best ability to think, lead, influence and change. As the bridge between the Visionary and Managers and Frontliners, the Driver flows the vision from the former to the latter and brings it to life. Assertive and empathetic in equal measure, the Driver drives themselves and others to make their workplace change program a success.

When hired to implement a Link:Flow:Grow overhaul, in the early stages we model best practices as your external Driver while helping you to identify or hire your internal Driver, then train them to drive ongoing success.

Where most people get it wrong in real life is juggling future-focused Driver activities with current-focused Manager ones. That's the fast track to burnout. Or, a successful Driver in a corporate environment may start their own business (where they should be the Visionary) but continue to perform Driver activities.

Sometimes, you may think you already have a Driver—but check carefully. You might be surprised what new perspectives you can gain when you nut out requirements.

The Manager

The Manager's role is to bring out the best in the Frontliners who perform day-to-day work. They are focused on the present. Whether the Manager is a division, department or section manager from any functional business unit, they all need to take the vision of the Visionary that is articulated by the Driver, and organise the who, what, when, where and how to make it happen.

To complement the right-brain focus of Visionaries and Drivers, left-brain-focused Managers mainly perform analytical and practical operational workplace functions.

A left-brain focus doesn't mean that Managers and Frontliners don't use their right-brain functions!

It means that their role is more to achieve day-to-day workplace tasks than come up with big-picture strategies. Strong Managers are often meticulous and have the in-depth operational knowledge and skills to motivate and mobilise large groups of people working complex equipment through best-practice processes.

A mentally unfit Manager can affect the performance and morale of the people working at and below the Manager's level of responsibility. Managers poorly managed by Drivers and above may suffer burnout if they are expected to perform a mix of Driver and Manager duties and thus lose focus and productivity.

If Managers are disconnected from the big picture, they could resent or even sabotage their managers, and lead subordinates poorly. If Managers are too focused on the details, or their org chart is not an IOC, they may micromanage Frontliners and end up spending their time executing Frontliner work—when they should step back and perform more managerial functions.

The Frontliner

Frontliners are present-focused frontline supervisors of small teams that execute day-to-day operational plans and tasks that usually use the left brain's analytical and practical functions. Anyone who interacts directly with customers in their day-to-day role is also a Frontliner.

Frontliners are not just mindless minions.

They definitely should not be treated like meat robots.

Yes, they may operate in small groups and take care of small areas of responsibility. They may focus on team and individual targets and goals, but they perform best when connected to the big picture (and are not siloed).

It is important that they have clear links of accountability to the leaders above them in the IOC, and have the peripheral Spidey sense to collaborate with other teams to fulfil the workplace goals of the Company, Team and Self.

Disempowered Frontliners are those who mistrust and feel unsupported by management, operate on their turf with their own personal agenda overriding company objectives, and are usually secretive or defensive when things go wrong. Time-bombs, in other words.

Individually, their impact may be small—but if you have a fair few rogue Frontliners, it is a symptom of a company's leadership problem (the fish rots from the head). The good news is, if it is a leadership problem, the solution also lies with leadership.

***

Visionary, Driver, Manager, Frontliner. Now that you've been introduced to the four leadership roles running the engine of workplace mental fitness, let's shed some light on how to create high-impact leaders in each role.

As you start connecting the dots on how to make it all work for your organisation and allow brighter and brighter insights to dawn on you, let's cast our eyes to the top of the HIL—High-Impact Leadership. In today's hyperconnected yet volatile, uncertain, complex and ambiguous world, your ability to adopt a new approach to leadership will determine how well you thrive in the future. Let's chat further about HIL climbs in the next chapter.

Mental Fitness Stretch

- Consider your reporting structure and identify who fulfils each leadership role.
- Who is fulfilling the wrong role, or multiple roles?
- Can you see if any roles are missing?
- How are these people performing and what needs to change?

Chapter 8

HIL climbs are worth the view

Perhaps life was simpler for managers one or two generations ago.

Back then, position was authority, and 'Do as I say, not as I do' leadership worked because workers obeyed it. Today's workforce know and assert their rights more than their predecessors did. It's only a problem for you as a leader if you think such an empowered workforce is trouble.

The truth is, you can get a lot more out of a thinking workforce if you know how to bring out their best.

If your leadership style is no longer getting you the results it used to, find out why. An excellent warm-up exercise is to watch the short animated video 'Who moved my cheese' based on the bestseller by Spencer Johnson.[15]

Today, effective leadership requires a different approach. The criteria have changed.

Welcome to the Conceptual Age

We've seen too many business leaders, managers and supervisors who are still using their old map to navigate the new territory. No wonder they're lost.

High-Impact Leadership (HIL) is required to meet the organisational demands of the Conceptual Age.

Workplace futurist Dan Pink suggests in his book *A Whole New Mind* that the Conceptual Age of creators and empathisers is rapidly replacing the Information Age of knowledge workers.[16]

This era is driven by a 'high-concept, high-touch' approach to managing people and organisations that results in High-Impact Leadership:

- **high concept** is the capacity to detect patterns and opportunities and to combine seemingly unrelated ideas into something new

- **high touch** involves the ability to manage oneself and empathise with others in the pursuit of purpose and meaning.

High Concept + High Touch = High-Impact Leadership

High-Impact Leadership (HIL) is contextual to one's area of responsibility and needed at every level of the organisation. In other words, Frontliner, Manager, Driver and Visionary leaders should all exercise HIL climbs.

If leaders do not achieve high impact, they will not be game changers. When we recruit and place managers to effect organisational change, they have to be top performers who exercise their IQ, EQ and CQ to achieve High-Impact Leadership.

In John's words: 'IQ is the understanding of what needs to be done and EQ is the wisdom of how to apply it.' CQ, or Collaborative Quotient, is a relatively new term that recognises the importance of working with the team in mind. This secret sauce flavours workplace interactions with mutual support and cooperation.

A mentally fit manager:

- is aware of their own emotional state

- is aware of others' emotional states

- is able to manage their own emotional state
- is able to manage others' emotional states.

The above is an easy way to understand renowned psychologist Daniel Goleman's model of emotional intelligence, which talks about regulating and recognising emotion in personal and social contexts.[17]

Purely 'high-concept' leaders exercising their IQ are more likely to rely on an intellectualised approach to management. For example, they may manage field staff from their office. They may have the best interests of the business at heart. They are definitely KPI- and goal-oriented. But without 'high touch', they miss the opportunity to connect with their people and inspire them to create change.

'High-touch' leaders exercising their EQ and CQ engage their people directly. They feel close to their people. They initiate discussions around continual improvement and change. Candidly, this may be to their own detriment because it gives them more work to do, but this increases their value as a leader. The benefit of this approach is that 'high touch' gets people to perform at higher levels willingly.

However, 'high touch' without 'high concept' can create happy shiny people who risk forgetting their business objectives. Management is a balancing act between high touch and high concept. The failure in this is getting too close to your staff. A professional relationship must be maintained. It can be nurturing, but it is not a social friendship.

Frontline managers need to develop both high concept and high touch; spend time in the office and in the field. If they cannot handle both zones of work, they will be outdone by step-ups who can.

Step-ups

We've spent a lot of time developing step-ups or emerging leaders. We spot promising workers in the field who demonstrate drive and energy, and train them to 'step up' and lead others.

Don't let their lack of MBAs fool you. Their effectiveness does not stem from degrees or diplomas. (Ironically, tertiary qualifications become obstacles when leading blue-collar teams. That's why we don't broadcast our paper qualifications. They get in the way of being seen as 'one of us' and managing successfully from the ground up.) As they grow professionally, step-ups succeed in implementing more and more mental fitness strategies into business operations because they 'get it'. They:

- know that to get the best from people, they need to be included in the team, as 'one of us'
- know the realities of work in the field
- work together in their teams to keep the cycle of continual improvement turning.

These step-ups will climb into Driver roles to drive future business success.

As a manager, you too can help your workforce succeed. Achieve better flow. Reduce burnout. Renouncing academic qualifications is a tactic. The crux of success is to build your own capacity to grow and develop your people's capabilities. Your key to success is to be and become a high-impact leader.

The HIL climb

Here are some milestones in the HIL climbs of different levels of leadership.

The high-impact Frontliner

A high-impact **Frontliner** adds value to the day-to-day operations of the business by ensuring productivity and efficiencies are gained through safe and reliable systems of work. They question the status quo if they have to, and shepherd success in their teams.

The high-impact Frontliner exercises:

- assertiveness $\times$ IQ $\times$ EQ $\times$ CQ
- effective communication strategies
- sound and reliable systems of work
- behavioural expectations
- contingency management strategies
- sound activity management techniques.

The high-impact Manager

A high-impact **Manager** uses strategy and tactics to ensure teams are prepared, resourced and competent. They add value by preparing the team strategy in advance and ensuring the right use of resources, people and focus.

The high-impact Manager exercises:

- advanced coping capacity
- planning and tactical approaches
- assertiveness $\times$ IQ $\times$ EQ $\times$ CQ
- decisive communication
- behavioural standards
- high expectation standards
- an understanding of the activity requirements.

The high-impact Driver

A high-impact **Driver** has already established the framework of success in which the teams operate. They have taken the plan and turned it into strategy, they have met with their key people and planned the actions. They have Visionary directives firmly established in their minds and can be relied on to apply financial and human resources to achieve the desired outcomes.

The high-impact Driver exercises:

- assertiveness $\times$ IQ $\times$ EQ $\times$ CQ
- engagement and teamwork
- high-concept, high-touch leadership
- high expectation standards
- uncompromising behavioural values
- decisiveness
- planning for profit strategies
- elite-level public speaking.

The high-impact Visionary

A high-impact **Visionary** is the owner/director who defines business expectations and works relentlessly on new plans and new opportunities for the organisation. They have very high expectations for a return on investment and put the right people with the right talent in the right roles.

The high-impact Visionary exercises:

- C-suite level IQ $\times$ EQ $\times$ CQ
- high-expectation approaches
- engagement of industry and talent experts
- the five-year plan as the business driver
- a vision for their business
- a set of behavioural values that will not be compromised
- discernment in conducting meetings that matter.

HIL's impact on 'battery' capacity

We use the batteries analogy (see figure 8.1) a lot at our workshops.

Why?

It relates to what high-impact leaders can achieve. It's an easy way to talk about *individual* mental fitness goals in concrete terms. Achieving these goals builds *collective* workplace mental fitness.

Figure 8.1: Mental fitness batteries

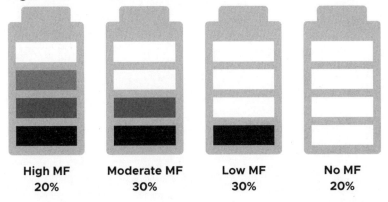

| High MF | Moderate MF | Low MF | No MF |
| 20% | 30% | 30% | 20% |

Transport, mining & manufacturing business stats (2008–present)

This is not meant to be labelling for labelling's sake. Different mental fitness (MF) profiles respond to different types of intervention.

Suppose you could charge a person like you charge a mobile phone. When you connect them to the power source you see the percentage of mental fitness battery power they possess.

We've worked 2 million hours with workplace groups and teams over ten years. Our data suggests four individual mental fitness profiles, as shown in table 8.1 (overleaf).

Table 8.1: Battery level mental fitness profiles

Individual mental fitness	% of people at the start	Intervention needed
High MF	20%	20 per cent are mentally fit irrespective of work culture. These people are great to work with and self-motivated to achieve great things in their role.
Moderate MF	30%	30 per cent are moderately mentally fit and can excel in the right environment. They need the business to be part of their success story.
Low MF	30%	30 per cent have low mental fitness and struggle with their roles. Working with them is like riding a roller coaster: they are very good one day and not so good the next. They need training to become balanced and mentally fit.
No MF	20%	20 per cent have no mental fitness. They're characterised by very self-focused needs and struggling to connect with business and team objectives if they conflict with self. They can be trained in some cases but also may need a job intervention.

Ideally, you'd shift the ratios to 30/60/10/0 after three to six months with Link:Flow:Grow intervention. It can be done. These figures are based on our strike rate.

Here's a quick way to assess how mentally fit or unfit someone is. Table 8.2 shows how you can start with your managers.

Table 8.2: Mental fitness assessment

	Mentally unfit manager	Mentally fit manager
Response	Emotional (creates drama), aggressive, blaming, shifts goalposts, stonewalls	Calm, assertive, encouraging, clear, manages expectations well, focuses on positives
Results	Adds to negativity of issues, or has no positive impact on issues	Creates positivity, and changes negative to positive ASAP
Leadership rating	Ineffective, short-term gains, reactive, poor	Effective, long-term gains, excellent

Success collaborators

Workplace mental fitness is of no value without the business being profitable and efficient. Success should not require the Visionary to work at a level lower than their title.

To support the internal work of high-impact leaders at all levels of an organisation, be sure to appoint external professionals as shown in table 8.3.

Table 8.3: External professionals to support HIL

External professional	Purpose
Great business/insurance advisers	To set mental fitness and mental health as priorities and still run a fabulous business.
Great mental fitness adviser	To focus on a culture of engagement and resilience.
Great mental health adviser	To ensure all staff have available support in the mental health area.

Workplace mental fitness is the consequence of appointing the right people to drive the business forward, putting the right procedures into place, and operating a collegial, Safe System of Work that truly promotes individual health and wellbeing.

What's important about being collegial? When you allow the workforce to share responsibility and authority, and when the environment rewards cooperation and collaboration instead of internal competitiveness, everyone wins.

When you come across a mentally fit work environment, you will be staggered by its awesomeness and how well it is accepted by the workforce.

The HIL climbs of High-Impact Leadership may require ongoing effort from all leaders, yet you will find all the effort worth it. The views from the peak of success are spectacular.

We've just covered the leaders who are the agents of flow, and the amazing impact they can have on workforce capacity.

Such leaders are highly prized in notoriously complex projects involving both blue- and white-collar workers. In the next chapter, we explore how a whole-brain approach helps you achieve success even in the most trying situations, especially 'multi-tone workplaces'.

Mental Fitness Stretch

- Consider those in your organisation who work at different leadership levels: do they match up?

- How much micromanagement has to happen because of ineffective leadership?

- Does your Driver drive the success of the organisation?

Chapter 9
Whole-brain leadership in multi-tone organisations

In chapter 7 we touched briefly on the concepts of left-brain and right-brain thinking. Now we'll explore practical ways that whole-brain thinking can improve leadership impact.

Let's start with an example of a white-collar decision that assumes that its impact is the same on both white- and blue-collar workers. Imagine if the four-day work week becomes law. Higher income white-collar workers can afford to take that extra day off. They spend the time on self-care and leisure pursuits, and improve their quality of life.

Lower-income blue-collar workers cannot afford to do the same. They need to clock enough paid hours to make ends meet. They end up taking extra jobs on the side just to keep going. Hello, burnout.

A mentally fit leader who appreciates whole-brain thinking would not make such a decision. Essentially, managers who appreciate whole-brain thinking are more successful in leading and managing people who don't think a lot like them.

First, we distinguish between two types of workplaces: it is easier for managers to get through to their people in a single-tone organisation than in a multi-tone one.

A typical **single-tone** organisation is made up of white-collar professionals based indoors in office buildings. The workforce tends to be well-educated and comfortable when presented with abstract concepts. For example, an accounting firm or software company.

A typical **multi-tone** organisation is made up of white- and blue-collar workers working indoors and outdoors. For example, a construction company or courier company. The challenges of managing a multi-tone business are compounded by the presence of different demographics and values, and some groups don't trust each other to begin with. There is a strong tendency to equate net worth with self-worth, and this is especially damaging in a multi-tone business.

There is a need for higher mental fitness in managers to ensure cultural cohesion across a multi-tone organisation. There are more complex socio-cultural contours to deal with in a multi-tone organisation if you want to flow the nourishing waters of workplace mental fitness across the entire landscape.

Two ways to be an effective whole-brain leader are to abolish the idea of 'human capital', and to stop thinking of averages when it comes to people.

Abolish human capital

Yes, we're prepared that some of you might get upset and invite you to think deeper about what this term means.

As managers, we must work with employees of all backgrounds to achieve their mental peak. We must not treat them like human cattle (or the more sanitised business term, 'human capital'). Put people first, and the profits shall follow.

'Human capital' sounds really important but what does it really mean? Oxforddictionaries.com defines 'Capital' as 'wealth in the form of money or other assets owned by a person or organisation or available for a purpose such as starting a company or investing.'[18]

As an employee, you, friend, are viewed as something, not someone, that makes itself available to make others rich. You're owned.

We want to make sure the nuances of 'owned' are not lost on you, because that means organisations win in this relationship.

'Human capital' sends the wrong message. It is a management concept based on averages and the lack of regard for the individual human beings it's talking about.

Its interest is in the use of humans to produce profit, human needs be damned. It naturally breeds human disconnect.

Successful managers and leaders in the Conceptual Age will fail if they continue to see people as human capital and treat them accordingly.

Challenge what's average

So how do you do that, especially in multi-tone businesses?

Author Todd Rose argues in his book *The End of Average* that there's no such thing as an average human and we shouldn't base our organisations and government policies on it.[19]

What we need is whole-brain thinking and whole-brain leadership. In his book *A Whole New Mind* Dan Pink wrote that the ones who shall rule the future use their right brain as well as their left.[20]

Ned Herrmann's validated research on whole-brain thinking[21] goes further, suggesting four brain quadrants. It explains the paradox of why people can be extremely clever and dumb at the same time—for example, the absent-minded genius. More importantly, it creates an awareness of your own thinking preferences, an appreciation of others' patterns (especially if they're very different from your own), and the ability to act outside your default mode.

Essentially, Herrmann discovered that the brain has four main ways of perceiving and processing information: Analytical and Practical thinking in the rational left brain, and Relational and Experimental in the intuitive right brain. Herrmann suggests that individuals, teams and organisations use the whole-brain thinking model to unlock better thinking and leverage the full spectrum of thinking preferences.

We're now in the messy stage of transitioning to whole-brain thinking.

Futurists and business leaders are looking for answers to the problems brought about by thinking with half a brain for too long; the Knowledge Age of the past 50 years has valued logical and analytical left-brain thinking. We are evolving into the Conceptual Age, which combines left-brain thinking with creative and empathetic right-brain thinking.

The 'whole new mind' approach to moving from good to great means management needs to shift to a person-focused approach while still running their organisations. This will in fact let you run them a lot better.

Businesses that are successful in building rapport with every member of the organisation will tap into a fabulous reserve. Help your managers build workplace mental fitness with whole-brain thinking, teach them assertiveness to champion change, and help them understand what the business plan needs. In essence, help them build more successful teams.

As you master the art of whole-brain thinking, you become more effective in becoming a high-impact leader who leads with clarity and inspires high performance in what's now a mentally fit workplace. The next chapter gives Visionaries some tips on how to do this.

Mental Fitness Stretch

- What are the concepts behind whole-brain thinking?

- Do you have whole-brain thinkers or a bunch of lefties and/or righties?

- Consider your most uncomfortable thinking mode and how it affects your daily process. (Kris confesses he is most impatient if he has to be in Analytical and Practical organisation mode, as he would much rather be exercising Relational and Experimental thinking in strategy and disruption. John is brilliant in Analytical and Practical mode and prefers that to Relational and Experimental thinking. Alexis switches among the four quadrants or combines one or more of them depending on what she's doing, for what purpose, and whom she's collaborating with.)

Chapter 10
The culture rots from the head

An organisation's most senior leader is entirely responsible for its existing culture. In Link:Flow:Grow, that person is the Visionary.

Organisational culture creates the outcomes, positive or negative. If your company is not overseen by a group of directors, then its culture and character rest on the shoulders of your most senior leader.

Too many business owners and leaders don't get this. They say 'Hey, come in and help me fix the problems out there amongst my people.' They get upset when it's suggested that they are a major part of the problem. We say they should celebrate, because this means they are part of the solution too. Because the culture rots from the head.

If you are that senior business leader who believes culture depends on the people in an organisation, and not you, please return this book and get your money back.

Don't self sabotage

An aspiring disciple once asked a Zen master how long it would take him to gain enlightenment if he joined the temple.

'Ten years,' said the Zen master.

'That's too long. What if I really work hard and double my effort?'

'Twenty years.'

When a business owner or director gets us to come in and fix their problems, they may unwittingly sabotage the process by doing one of two things, or both:

1. Stepping into the day-to-day tasks involved in the transition.

2. Doing what they've always done while expecting different results.

As the Visionary, you don't need to be the Driver. What you do need is to set clear directives, then step back with trust and respect, and let your people fulfil their roles. Let them exercise their mental fitness muscles.

The Visionary's job is to do the following:

- Set clear Key Result Areas (KRAs).

- Expect the business structure to set clear KPIs (Key Performance Indicators) for every role in the organisation.

- Provide wisdom and navigation to the business during tough times.

- Clarify what success looks like.

If you don't do a good job clarifying these areas, it's self-sabotage. Like setting demolition charges to your house while you're renovating it. Without an IOC, it's easy for things to slip through the cracks. Like identifying skill gaps, but not following up with a training program. Or letting someone do a job they don't understand.

The 100 per cent commitment required to build better mental fitness also includes the moral courage to review the role you play in influencing the state of your organisation. Review your org chart for 'demolition charges' where a senior manager may be sabotaging their subordinates' performance through micromanaging or other means.

Do this without consequences (condemn the action, not the person), then make a determined effort as a business to lay no more damaging charges. No more saboteurs!

How to set yourself up for failure

Our greatest failures up to now were in organisations where Visionaries messed things up.

They neither established the right structure nor appreciated how important their behaviour was to success. Or, they'd let us come in, start redesigning their organisation, and once the first results started to trickle in, they'd swoop in and do something based on their old paradigm, which threatened to wipe out all the progress we made with their people. Having the highest authority in the organisation also means having the potential to do the greatest damage if you are being a dimwit.

My (Kris's) expertise on dimwits comes from having been a spectacular one myself. Many times. During my young and cocky days, I'd do the wrong thing over and over again, and stubbornly think I knew it all. 'Don't tell me how to run my company. Who needs training? I know what I'm doing.' I was pretty well schooled by my spectacular failure with people and results.

When asked the question 'Why is the staff turnover so high?', dimwitted leaders would answer 'That's because we haven't found the right people.'

Wrong answer.

The next section explains why.

Value leaching

We learnt the hard way that placing shining stars in a mentally unfit work environment can be detrimental to their brilliance.

It's not that we haven't found the right people. The right people leave because the work environment does not bring out their best.

It would be a disaster if the talent subsequently started questioning their own competence after spending time in a workplace environment that does not support them to function at their Human Performance Optimum.

In our experience, people who start out as mentally fit in a mentally unfit workplace usually come to a crunch after 12 months. The horizontal bars in figure 10.1 are the boundaries of workplace mental fitness of the organisation as a whole at the time.

Figure 10.1: The impact of toxic workplace culture on individual mental fitness

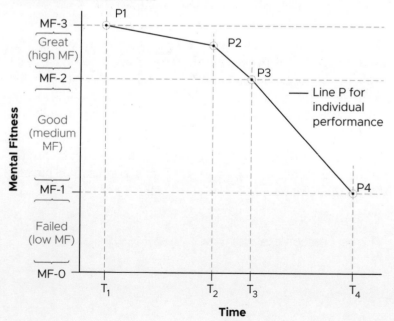

- The high achiever starts out at point P1 with high personal mental fitness and is largely immune to workplace toxicity until they hit crunch point P2, typically after 6 to 12 months.

- If they stay, their mental fitness and performance nosedives from P2 to P3. Most high performers would leave or quit at time T2 or slightly after.

- If they stay, they can be dragged down by the environment to hit a low of point P4.

If good staff keep leaving and there is rampant absenteeism or presenteeism, don't be too quick to blame the individuals involved. Check for deeper issues.

Do you see yourself in any of the following behaviours?

- Suddenly micromanaging managers by insisting that all purchases be approved by you, the business director.

- Loudly reprimanding a worker who has made a mistake in front of their coworkers.

- Boasting about your success and essentially saying 'Why can't you just be like me?'

- Giving your Driver a key accountability list, then telling them how you want things done.

- Condemning the person and not the behaviour when things go wrong.

- Taking credit for success and not acknowledging your people when things go right.

- Punishing failure instead of using it as a great opportunity for review, training and improvement.

- Sweating the small stuff, exploding at individual incidents instead of taking positive actions to advance big-picture goals.

Well, stop it.

We'll help you.

How to set yourself up for success

What this book recommends isn't something that can be done half-heartedly. This doesn't mean it will be hard all the way. It does mean that you must start with the right intention to lead all other leaders in the business to the right place by your example.

When you accept full responsibility for the state of your organisation, you reclaim your true power as well, by:

- leading yourself before leading others
- developing the determination to improve, learn, unlearn, relearn
- not being frustrated by failure and focusing on turning things around with training
- condemning the mistake, not the person making it
- setting managers up for success by training, being humble and setting the business on the right path.

During tough moments, the business will look to its highest level of leadership for direction. For hope and inspiration.

Empty mission and value statements won't cut it.

When it comes to guiding principles that must be manifested as concrete actions, these are the non-negotiables:

- trust
- respect
- success
- mental fitness
- unity
- resilience
- discipline.

You are not exempted because you're the boss.

The true grit of mental fitness is to make sure the non-negotiables are enforced. If we say we are going to do something, that's what gets done.

What gets in the way of things getting done is blind tolerance.

What is blind tolerance?

An example would be accepting negativity in the workplace. It's more about being pleasantly fake and pretending to get along, instead of facing and tackling the tough things.

'Zero Tolerance of BS' is our motto. Define your business beliefs and steadfastly reinforce them. People will respect you for it as it defines the company's core. We have too many values and mission statements that are meaningless other than to tick a 'we've done that' box.

There is nothing worse than shallow promises. Back them up with guts and honesty. Demonstrate that you are a leader who truly considers your people to be important, and you will reap the rewards every day.

No shortcuts to a winning culture

The playing field of achievement is not level; it slopes down towards the negative. If you do nothing about workplace culture, it backslides.

The ability to arrest this slide and keep moving upstream to the positive is a measure of High-Impact Leadership (HIL).

Developing mental fitness in organisations feels like hard work sometimes, because it requires constant attention. You and your organisation are either working towards mental fitness or sliding away from it. It's like your golf swing. Without constant practice, you'll find it harder and harder to keep it on track.

Once you've decided to plant mental fitness in your organisation, be patient. Give it the ongoing attention it needs to grow, then sit back and allow growth to happen. You can't rush it.

Are you still with us? It's a lot to take in, we know. No-one likes change, especially when you're being asked to change something about yourself! But we're just warming up.

You need to follow through if you want things to change. To build a bridge from where you are to where you want to be, you must have a Driver in place.

The Driver is not only the bridge builder, but also the person who must ensure that the workplace environment remains mentally fit. Let's explore this further in the next chapter.

Mental Fitness Stretch

- Does your board of directors appreciate the impact of mental fitness and the importance of workplace culture?

- Do your directors in general believe the 'culture rots from the head'?

- Can you identify where you are setting yourself, your teams and your organisation up for failure? How can you set yourselves up for success?

- What are your company's non-negotiables?

Chapter 11
Hello Driver, how's the weather?

What's your picture-perfect day? Sun shining, birds chirping and the air crisp and fresh? Sounds good, doesn't it, but what on earth does this have to do with this book?

Well, a lot, actually.

The key weatherperson in an organisation is the Driver. The Driver:

- has a bird's eye view of the environment and observes the fluctuations in conditions
- is always up to date with the weather and providing feedback and options for the business to achieve the ideal work environment
- knows how to anticipate and ride out bad weather. They know what to do when serious issues (cyclones) are about to hit.

An environment that is mentally fit will be stable and clear whereas the mentally unfit environment will be unstable and have storm clouds on the horizon. The mentally unfit environment can erode the employees' belief in the business and its future.

The Driver also understands the need for the business to appreciate fine, calm weather and songbirds, and strives to make the environment perform at its optimal.

Yes, a tough ask, yet it is critical to the business and teams.

The ten capabilities of the Driver

As the Driver of organisational change to create a high-performance workforce, you need to wear many hats. The Driver is accountable for profit, people and progress in the organisation.

We've shortlisted the top capabilities to look out for when identifying or hiring a Driver.

1. Activates shared vision and values

Getting to a shared vision is sometimes not easy, especially for the task-focused, time-poor soldier ants in the organisation who will be executing the plan. The Driver:

- builds and sells the vision convincingly; the more effort that is put into the plan in the beginning, the easier it is for people to get it

- nurtures and restructures using the continuous improvement process, so it actually starts to build momentum and take shape.

2. Operationalises the organisation's strategic plan

This is where the Intelligent Org Chart and its KPIs become key drivers to turn strategy into operational success. The Driver must be able to see the plan in these important documents.

The Driver transfers important elements and sub-elements into KPIs and works with everyone involved to bring about individual success, which in turn builds operational success.

3. Provides twenty-first-century HIL

High-Impact Leadership (HIL) is the only way to avoid excuses and time-wasting. There may be a number of elements that need rework to create better linkages and then flow. In many cases these bottlenecks need to be removed. One single bottleneck can strangle a whole plan: HIL can see the bottlenecks, negotiate the solutions and create the flow.

4. Prioritises key deliverables

You have to learn to crawl before you walk. Many IOC audits reveal there is no soul or vision, and without it mental fitness will never live long and prosper. While there may be opportunities to tweak the current plan, working on establishing a culture through senior management and getting them to own it is key.

Prioritise items in clusters as some can be worked concurrently. Items such as succession planning and high-level HR planning can be a consequence of other softer, more creative elements being implemented. Some things occur as a natural progression—look for them.

5. Builds reliable teams

The Driver building the culture and environmental acceptance of how the teams work is just the beginning: managers then build, nurture, coach and mentor, and let the Frontliners get on with business. Frontliners play a key role in sustaining the flow in the teams.

An effective team is built from a sound strategy and directives must flow from the top down, so results can flow from the team back to the senior leadership.

Never underestimate the worth of great Frontliners and Managers in this process. Drivers harness their energy and enthusiasm or, if they don't have it, find someone who does.

6. Exercises high assertiveness and emotional intelligence

In every project we have worked on, the elements of passiveness and assertiveness have played a star role. Mental fitness does not need 'yes' men. People need to speak up to challenge the status quo and introduce change.

Leaders in the business need to regard speaking up as a positive and encourage assertiveness expressed with emotional intelligence. If your Drivers build these key components and use them wisely, you will be blown away by the results.

7. Exemplifies and creates workplace mental fitness

Ahhh, the flow of mental fitness: you can smell it in the air, you can see it in the people and their outputs. We often in this book ask you to stand back and look for it, and we cannot stress how important this is because if you can't see it, you haven't got it. Change starts with the Visionary. They must be able to see the flow of what they want to create; then they will see the bottlenecks and work to solve the issues they create. When Visionaries have great Drivers to take this journey with them, they will happily help to identify better ways of doing things.

8. Communicates with assertiveness and respect

Many of the blue-collar workers we see may not be polished Rhodes scholars, but they are valuable too. Drivers nurture their grit and guts to tell it like it is without being negative and inward-looking. As a result workers learn to communicate, say what they mean and not be afraid of the consequences. You can't question the status quo without courage, and you can't build respect from your peers if you don't give it yourself. Drivers demonstrate that everyone has a role and an opinion; it's how you handle it that makes the difference.

9. Exercises whole-brain thinking

Whole-brain thinking gets you to use the weaknesses in your thinking preferences and turn them into strengths. Drivers:

- encourage the deskbound quiet achiever to step forward and be confident about sharing their opinion

- remind the outspoken 'don't tell me how to suck eggs' types that they are a part of the greater good and the world does not revolve around them

- encourage their workforce to stretch beyond their habits and help us all to practise whole-brain leadership.

10. Uses the IOC to achieve all of the above

Everything is focused on the Link:Flow:Grow plan. The IOC will have highlighted the issues and the Visionary will have endorsed the journey. Achieving the goals in the plan is critical, because once we have achieved it, guess what: we can do it all again. Mental fitness creates more mental fitness. It's a living breathing cultural thing created in the IOC that set the standards for success.

***

Every business needs a Driver to develop the mental fitness they need to survive: to keep an eye on the weather in the business, because not all days will be plain sailing. There will be times of turbulence and some outright scary storms that will all need to be managed accordingly. With the right people, the responsibility and authority to complete a successful journey are shared. We should not expect that there'll be sunshine and roses every day, because things will change.

After linking best practice processes and resources, and flowing workplace mental fitness with High-Impact Leadership, we have planted the seeds for phenomenal business growth. Growth is the result of achieving EveryBest by exercising workplace mental fitness.

Next, let's look at what naturally flourishes when Grow is done right:

- Growth is achieved on the backs of each employee giving their best each and every day.

- Long-term excellence is not just discussed, it is maintained, and the business begins to flourish.

Mental Fitness Stretch

- How's the weather (corporate culture) at your workplace?

- How do you monitor the weather there?

- Are your weather monitors (management) trained and capable rainmakers?

- Are you proactively narrowing gaps with training?

- Or are you doing nothing until you get hit by a cyclone?

Chapter 12
EveryBest
in action

Have you ever met a 'MaxWell Mind'? It's someone who performs at their peak without distraction or hesitation. They have great alertness and mental agility. These are people fully immersed in whatever they are great at doing.

It always amazes us when we meet these people. It's not about the job they're doing, it's about the connection of the mind. They are in the zone, not just once or twice but seemingly all the time.

Everyone doing their best: is that a fantasy or can it really exist in reality? The quest for being the best never ends and your organisation is either moving towards being the best or away from it.

The most anyone can give on any given day is ... their best.

The value of EveryBest

An organisation functions at its EveryBest when every single person is performing at their Human Potential Optimum, or peak mental fitness. Collectively, the high workplace mental fitness creates a high-performance team without signs of negativity, absenteeism, presenteeism and burnout.

Most of us have probably been involved with a project or two that turned out really well, and we were proud of our success and maybe even celebrated it. That's the same feeling as being part of the journey that turns mayhem into mental fitness.

Look at the prize you earn for bravely working through all the changes required of you and the people you lead! With every person and system at their EveryBest and the business now functioning with Flow and Grow, what satisfaction that must give. This is a peak performance state, and the feeling of wonder you experience when someone is performing at their EveryBest is palpable and extremely rewarding.

EveryBest is as good as it gets.

You can appreciate now why mental health and other wellbeing initiatives can Flow and Grow much better through a mentally fit business. In high-stress, high-demand businesses this is so important because it means people can now sleep at night, safety incidents and stress are minimised, and a vibrant collaborative culture now exists that was never there before. Be diligent about who you select for each role and be even more protective to guard the culture you have grown and developed.

When was the last time someone took your breath away? I (Kris) am amazed by the singer Mandy Harvey (watch her on YouTube when you have the chance). She is truly fabulous. We may think only extraordinary feats such as this inspire such wonder and delight, but the ability to work successfully 12 hours a day in a job that is potentially tedious and mind numbing with flow is just as amazing.

Three phases of achievable workplace excellence

There is no end point to growing a high-performance culture. No matter how well you are doing now, the key is to ask yourself as a business leader, 'Could I do even more?' If not, then you have the right intent and should be respected for that. If you could do more, seek leaders in this space, get your business reviewed and set your business on the path to be the best in this space. There is no perfection but there is definitely best practice. A business review will give feedback that either you:

- need to do better and these are the focal points, or

- are doing great and you need to maintain it.

Either way, you know and can comfortably report this to your organisation's board or leadership committee.

Let us stretch your imagination further with a three-stage map of success a Link:Flow:Grow system can create. This map is accurate. It gets you where you want to go.

Phase 1: Redesign the workplace using the IOC

Create a roadmap for achieving the high-performance workplace culture we call EveryBest (Band 10), by addressing the nine bands or business-critical functions that are its foundations. (This is discussed in depth in chapter 6.)

This includes a full business audit using the IOC (discussed in chapter 5), as well as gap assessment and training on the four progressive leadership roles (discussed in chapter 7).

Phase 2: Establish workplace mental fitness

When Band 10 is established, the organisation operates in a new mentally fit mode that provides the best environment for optimising mental health in its people, and supports them to perform at their EveryBest.

Managers will have reduced the stressors resulting from poor management, and demonstrated that they can influence the state of mental health in their workforce without putting everything into the too-hard basket and dumping it on the psychologists.

Mental health issues occur in a spectrum, and a mentally fit workplace takes care of all but the most serious mental health issues.

Phase 3: Establish workplace mental health

By now, your mentally fit organisation is humming along being fabulous. Phase 2 has taken care of the mental health issues that have responded well to great management and workplace mental fitness. If anyone experiences any other chronic or acute mental health issues, they can be put into the care of mental health experts such as psychologists and counsellors.

As part of performance management, proactive mental health training can also be introduced at this phase, such as mindfulness training, resilience training, or specific programs for anxiety, depression, anger management or burnout.

Is EveryBest achievable?

Everyone doing their best — is that a fantasy or can it exist in reality?

The statistics show that EveryBest is currently a fantasy. But with Link:Flow:Grow you can make it a reality.

PwC estimates that every dollar invested in creating a mentally healthy workplace will reward the organisation with a return on investment (ROI) of 2.3.[22] We estimate that the Link:Flow:Grow workplace mental fitness program can easily reap an ROI of 10.

In an EveryBest organisation guided by the IOC, amazing things can happen as the culture supports the pursuit of bringing out everyone's best. That's an organisation worth working for — one with integrity and pride of ownership.

With this chapter on EveryBest, we conclude part I, in which we outlined the key concepts of the Link:Flow:Grow system that enable your organisation to become MindFit for work.

Next, in part II, we invite you to listen in on the real-life issues from our consulting work that have been most relatable to other organisations. We encourage you to apply our toolkit to your own workplace, and reflect on our insights to explore which are most relevant to you.

Mental Fitness Stretch

- How do you know the mental fitness of your workplace?

- How could your business make its people feel great about what they do, and stay efficient and productive?

- What would EveryBest look like at your workplace?

- Are your wellness and psychological care programs stacking up against business scrutiny?

PART II
Making It Real

We trust you've found part I eye opening. (Great if you've been entertained as well!)

Part II is where the fun really starts. Stories! Action! The spotlight is on you.

In workplaces everywhere, for far too long there has been chaos brought about by thinking with half a brain. Futurists, business leaders and mental health professionals continue to seek answers to complex workplace challenges with wide-ranging impacts, sometimes fatal.

We have many of the answers. We'll help you make the MindFit link to create a kickass workforce that achieves long-term business excellence.

At the time of writing, our work has had an impact on hundreds of managers and thousands of workers across many companies in four high-risk industries (construction, transport, mining and manufacturing).

We'd like to share these answers with you.

In part II, here's what you get in each chapter:

- **Story:** one or more real-life encounters or workplace challenges based on a theme.
- **Toolkit:** what practical actions we took to provide solutions.
- **Insights:** our learning outcomes and how you could apply them too.

This is not meant to be a DIY 12-step program. It is an introduction to what we have achieved and what you could possibly achieve by applying our approach.

Enjoy the stories. If you see something familiar, then delve deeper into the toolkit. Tap into our insights. Let it integrate. Use our roadmaps to guide you on what to start doing and what to stop doing, what to do first and what to do later.

Let's start with the IOC.

Chapter 13

The IOC: A beacon for change

This story is about a company that risked losing a multimillion-dollar contract due to serious safety incidents. The tools we used were the IOC, gap assessments and prioritisation.

And we learned that audits can never be too over the top.

Story: Undoing manufacturing mayhem

A manufacturing giant was in trouble and asked for John's help. A number of serious safety incidents at a customer's worksite had put their multimillion-dollar contract in jeopardy. Their industry reputation was at risk.

There was a pall of confused frustration hanging over the whole workforce because the proverbial left hand did not know what the right hand was doing. Departments and teams worked in silos; there was a blame culture and no mental fitness champion to make it stop. Stupid money-wasting and time-wasting happened as a result.

The way things were actually done didn't match how they were supposed to be done on paper. A number of leadership and communication elements were holding the whole company back.

Toolkit

Armed with the IOC, I (John) audited the company and found a plethora of issues contributing to the chaos. Together with other tools and resources I identified all the main issues that needed work. A vomit bucket list, so to speak.

The company did not have a change champion or Driver to lead the transformation, so our consultant played the role of external Driver and culture building champion. I conducted gap assessments with staff and the leadership team to build a detailed profile of each person's skills and productivity blocks, including their 'high-concept, high-touch' leadership score. A large number of issues were itemised, clustered and prioritised. (Good prioritisation helped to identify the key changes and many of the others just fell into place behind them.)

Used this way, the IOC is a powerful beacon for change because issues are translated into KPIs and targets for every level of the organisation to work on.

To improve workplace mental fitness:

- Audit your entire organisation in the key business areas of the 10 Bands using the IOC. Release the report to key managers and follow up, follow up, follow up.

- Be ruthless, as the initial audit can never be too over the top. If you don't have the environment for people to excel in, you will never build the workplace mental fitness required to create a high-performance culture.

- Encourage a small number of critical changes to be driven from the top. Our results show that even a small number of these changes can have a dramatic effect on output, especially when they are driven from the top and performance expectations are applied to all levels of the organisation.

To ensure an effective IOC audit:

- Make time; don't rush the process.

- Ensure enough key players (Drivers, Managers, Frontliners) sit through the process to get a clear picture of the issues.

- Treat the audit report as a live document and keep adding to it if needed.

- Clarify how any proposed changes will be communicated.

- Conduct mini audits (gap assessments) on all key blue-collar or operational staff so the issues can either be consolidated against what has already been found, or can be added to the list.

- Cluster the issues into like groups and prioritise their rollout.

- Disseminate KPIs and targets to all levels of the organisation.

- Identify the people who need to be trained and/or coached.

Insights

Garbage in, garbage out—an audit can never be too over-the-top.

Accept that the cultural failures are coming from the leadership. The culture is rotten at the head so until this is understood the business will continue to make the same mistakes over and over again.

With so much effort for such little return, mayhem is in charge. The business needs to minimise the negatives and genuinely engage in mental fitness.

Ready for your first mental fitness workout? Here's a checklist to get you started.

My Mental Fitness Checklist

- Get your current org chart and match the roles against specific KPIs and business goals. Are the chart and the goals in alignment?

- Create an IOC.

- Define your business goals.

- What roles will help the organisation achieve the goals?

- What is each role accountable for? What are non-negotiables and what are nice-to-haves?

- Map out what needs to happen for the organisation to function at EveryBest.

Chapter 14
Candy shells just don't satisfy

This story is about a crunch time that resulted from a failure to recruit a mentally fit workforce. The tools we used were to leverage the change champion, the system and the labour hire group. We learned that it's not enough to love what you do.

Story: Candy without a core

Have you ever been let down by a sure thing?

Suppose there's a plate of M&M's on the table. They're cheerful and multicoloured, beckoning, 'Eat me!'

You've had M&M's before. You know what to expect when you pop a handful in your mouth. You chomp down on them. Oh, that satisfying crunch! Crisp candy mashed up with solid chocolatey morsels bursting onto gleeful tastebuds.

Now what if the M&M's were hollow? They look like M&M's from the outside but there's no chocolate on the inside. You pop a handful in your mouth and chomp down on them, anticipating chocolate heaven.

Oh! The betrayal!

A mentally unfit organisation is like M&M's with no filling.

It looks good and it seems like nothing is wrong. Its people seem to be doing a good job. They fly under the radar until … things come to the crunch.

We once discussed the M&M's metaphor with a talent management group. They had just finished researching staff engagement in their own business and were shocked to find it surprisingly low. They didn't really know why and were continuing to perpetuate the issue.

This company was hiring people with low mental fitness and not training them to increase their mental fitness. Staff were slipping down undetected into Battery 4 (the No Mental Fitness category in figure 8.1), 'checking out' and eventually leaving.

A 'checked out' employee exhibits negativity to the company they work for, rigid time focus, limited communication and poor engagement. The company has to determine if they have any of these and ensure the root cause is resolved.

Toolkit

A sugar-coated organisation with only a candy shell can look good, but not be great. To build greatness, we used a dynamic IOC that:

- monitored the state of workplace mental fitness and progress statuses of KPIs
- introduced a competent Driver to manage the transition and develop an EveryBest culture
- put a Safe System of Work (or SSoW) into place
- reviewed the effectiveness of their alertness program

- mapped out one-on-one accountability and support relationships for every employee.

There should be minimal quality standards for everything, jobs and workers. The IOC audit benchmarks the mentally fit people you need to make things happen — they will create a profitable outcome and reduce the exposure to high claims and insurance costs that are often the result of a disengaged workforce.

To ensure your organisation is not just a hollow shell:

- Research what you really need to get out of your people, especially if you're in a high-risk, high-demand industry.

- Redesign your recruitment practices and job descriptions to get the right level of competency, or get a mentally fit recruitment agency to help.

- Recruit for aptitudes and attitudes in addition to skills and experience.

- Give your people ownership of systems and processes.

- Benchmark your organisation against others.

- Manage performance daily, not biannually or annually.

- Pick one structured system to coach your people. A good example is Click! Colours,[23] which uses whole-brain thinking to 'help people and teams build relationships quick, by understanding what makes people tick!'

Insights

Ten years of data collection helped us notice that resilience is getting lower and lower and causing a lot of issues. When more workers follow the 'do what you love' mantra, they are less likely to accept that there are parts of their job they will hate. And less likely to put in the positive effort and discipline to perform well at work.

'What's wrong with choosing a job you love?' you may ask. 'What's bad about refusing to settle for anything less than the best?'

To quote Mark Manson from his refreshing book, *The Subtle Art of Not Giving a F*ck*: 'The desire for more positive experience is itself a negative experience. And, paradoxically, the acceptance of one's negative experience is itself a positive experience.'

In fact, we think it is far better to advise people to seek work that adds value to society, before seeking work they love.

The Japanese concept of *ikigai* makes a great Band 4 (Managing 'In' Design) consideration. To create a workforce of mentally fit people, match their *ikigai*, or 'reason to live', with the roles you have available where the person is giving something the world needs that they love doing while being paid for it (the combination of the right profession, passion, mission and vocation).

If you find a labour hire group or executive recruiter who can find you reliable quality candidates, hallelujah. Worship and adore them for they shall be your organisation's salvation.

There is nothing more gut-churning than being let down by a promising candidate. A hollow sugar-coated shell malnourishes your organisation's reputation and standing. A lot is at stake.

It's time we expect better from labour hire groups. If they cannot supply mentally fit candidates, look elsewhere. If yours can deliver such stellar candidates, reward them and promote that as the expected norm.

Stop hiring employees with low or no mental fitness (Batteries 3 and 4). With those currently in your workforce, take ownership of their weaknesses, train them and look after them.

Ensure a Driver is present in the business. Conduct a gap assessment and if there isn't a Driver present, recruit one.

You'll find that getting recruitment right 'upstream' will make it easier to achieve effective mental fitness in designing key deliverables, organisational change and performance management.

My Mental Fitness Checklist

- Select key members of your leadership team. For each person, assess whether what they did this week or month aligned with their original job description.

- Link business goals to role requirements (without specific people in mind). Is the person currently in the role the best fit?

- Do you spot any discrepancies between KPIs and performance and the position profile for the role?

- This week, if something goes wrong, note the number of responses that provide excuses vs the number of responses that solve the issue to completion.

- Assess the mental fitness of your recruiters.

Chapter 15

The classic slow roll

This story is about a slow death roll and how to stop it. We used mental fitness tools to clarify deliverables, review the IOC and manage performance. We learned to understand change resistance and the dangers of slow rolling.

Story: Lena's slow rollers

Lena had lost a lot of major business contracts of late. She blamed the dive in commodity prices, rising costs and a sluggish economy. She'd been resistant to customer feedback that her staff were performing below expectations, and defended them fiercely.

Lena disregarded the feedback even though audits showed her company's compliance to legislative requirements had slipped.

When someone took the time to show Lena the evidence of her staff's poor performance and her inadequate leadership — all of which was losing her contracts — it was hard for Lena to digest.

In the end, she reluctantly admitted that her organisation needed an overhaul if it was going to stand tall in the industry. Lena called me in, and said, 'John, I need your help.' Lena told me the story, and asked how I would solve her problems.

I appraised four of Lena's so-called Drivers. All scored fairly low and had little or no impact on the performance of people in the field. Lena was running a company that had but 50 per cent proficiency in leadership. It was also outdated in its approach to technology use. Nobody who worked there had ever heard of mental fitness, and they were going backwards at a rapid rate.

These items were tabled as the primary evidence. Lena and I called in the auditors and had the workers compensation premium checked. The staff I interviewed did not paint a pretty picture for Lena.

With all this information, we sketched a detailed picture of the state of mental unfitness in the business. From there, I separated the wheat from the chaff, ranked their priorities, mapped their actions, set milestones, and put it all together in a plan.

Lena reluctantly talked to the staff who weren't achieving the desired outputs and together with me set about recruiting a new Driver through a mentally fit recruiter. They put a coaching program in place to build and develop more proficient Frontliners and Managers, and future Drivers.

Their plan could now clearly show the key deliverables and quality protocols the organisation needed to become an industry leader.

With lots of input from Lena, I designed an IOC, implemented Link:Flow:Grow arrangements to track their action plans, and provided KPIs for each leader.

I felt gooood. What a successful outcome! All smiles. Enthusiastic handshakes.

'Thanks for coming! This mental fitness stuff is exactly what we need right now. Brilliant work! We'll get cracking on what's planned, based on our Intelligent Org Chart. And start looking for a Driver.'

Five weeks later … crickets.

It was very upsetting to my ego that these people were not engaged about changing. The program was destined to fail.

How unreasonable for them to agree with me, yet have no intention of actually making anything happen. I had been hit by a pleasantly fake response.

One of the keys to ensuring that mental fitness becomes part of an organisation's culture is combating slow rolling.

I refused to let this fail! I explained to Lena that it was unacceptable for the managers to drag their feet and slow roll the program. I suggested that they be counselled and that expectations be ramped up.

Fascinating! Once the managers were called out on their behaviour, the problem quickly disappeared.

Lena was happy. We now meet every month after their directors' meeting to plan for the coming month.

It was a brave step for Lena, and a necessary one for business survival. The slowest of rolls can be changed if real steps are put in place, starting from the top.

Toolkit

We redesigned key deliverables, reporting flow, and the performance management protocol to fight slow rolling. We redefined expectations, traced the sources of failures, and had more frequent performance management conversations.

To prevent slow rolling:

- Manage performance frequently; give your people timely bite-sized feedback and manageable change tasks.

- Introduce accountability.

- Study the IOC and where failure is coming from; prune your structure if required.

- Identify the bottlenecks and deal with them.

- Link roles to business goals, and flow mental fitness practices into all parts of the workforce.

- Learn to deliver negative information with more emotional intelligence.

- Don't evaluate people on things that are not clearly set.

- Find game changers at every level; make them your champions and give them the authority and resources to infect others with their enthusiasm.

- Surround yourself with people who can get you the results you want.

- Celebrate even small wins as this feeds momentum towards success.

Insights

In-principle acceptance of a change program without true determination to take action for change will lead to a slow roll to failure.

The classic slow roll is like a disease that slowly eats away the motivation and character of people and creates a zombie-like state. Link:Flow:Grow is the zombie antidote.

Sometimes the hardest bit is recognising that you have a slow roll, especially while 'busy' (can you see us roll our eyes) fighting fires. Conduct an IOC audit and you will soon find out why the slow roll exists.

Change often has a bad reputation in organisations. People hate change because it *is* a lot of trouble. But they need to wake up. Businesses are in a state of change every day, so those who resist change are delusional.

You owe it to yourself, your people and your business to find out how to release that resistance, and channel that energy into progressing solutions.

As Professor Gary Martin, the CEO of the Australian Institute of Management WA, boldly states, 'Those who don't embrace change cease to exist.' (If you want to start taking regular thought vitamins to get you used to this idea and others that inspire high performance, consider following Professor Martin on LinkedIn.)

The best organisations prepare their staff for change and grow because of it.

How does one resist the resistance to change? We have an A word for you: ALLOW it to happen. You may need to get curious about what's stopping the allowing; there could be powerful insights that come out of this to help you stop the slow rolling. Be courageous and enjoy exploring.

Slow rolling creates a whole lot of problems.

It creates stress and other mental illnesses. Remember that proverbial frog sitting in his pot as the water slowly heats up and threatens to make soup out of him? Don't let that be you. In some cases the slow roll has led to major health issues for Driver and Visionary level players: depression, irritability, foggy thinking, dulled instincts.

Everyone suffers as problems snowball. Slow rolling wears you down as more customers complain, people become complacent, activity gets out of alignment and insurance premiums rise. If these stressors affect the senior levels, then they also affect those at the lower levels who need to deal with emotional outbursts, negative comments and poor attitudes from their bosses.

Nothing moves forward, only backwards. When you agree to change and then don't embrace that change, you may think nothing is happening, but it is—only downhill. This behaviour is very torturous on staff and key people and is often a reason that people pack their bags and move on.

Brilliance is snuffed out. This is often the case in many smaller organisations that hire really good people but don't allow them to do things differently. They either shrink into their shells and stay under the radar or resign and move on.

The classic slow roll is like a cancer: the longer it is allowed to fester the worse it gets, even to the point where some business owners say that it can never be repaired. But there is a cure.

You can get results in as little as three months, and establish the foundations for a new world order in 12 to 24 months.

It takes a new broom to sweep clean. Put a great Driver champion and Link:Flow:Grow program in place and the cure is coming.

The great thing about the Link:Flow:Grow program is that once it is implemented, the slow roll is eliminated. Put a Driver in place to champion the program and things will move as fast as they practicably can.

My Mental Fitness Checklist

- Is there any evidence that you are scared to change the way you do business? Conduct an anonymous survey to find out.

- Conduct an audit to determine if your costs are high and you're having lots of incidents and issues. If you are, how are you going to deal with them?

- Review your insurance premiums and other operational costs. How might changing the way you work reduce them? Are there any research findings you could benchmark against?

Chapter 16

Build your people up

This story is about the merits of nurturing your workforce. The tools we used identified training gaps and closed them. Our learning was that no-one is static; people are dynamic and can always widen their skill set with new training.

Story: Making Shaun a superstar

I (Kris) can remember clearly the day I met Shaun. Shaun was very reserved and unassuming. He would shrink under scrutiny, but in the course of working with him, I saw his potential. He could be a bright, positive spark when he felt safe. He was an excellent operator, and was soon promoted to supervisor.

That's no small feat. After all, he was working in one of the largest mining companies in the world.

That's when I noticed his struggle. Shaun was smart but his poor English made him fear reports and emails. I encouraged him to study English, and it took Shaun one year to complete the course.

This grown man went back to the basics of spelling and grammar. He would do a spelling test each week. Before long, he was comfortable and confident enough to send text messages and emails in a business setting.

Shaun progressed to be a fine supervisor. He could showcase his true potential. There's nothing better than seeing someone shine.

It is a proud moment for the company to have achieved what it did with him. A leading company's showcase is built out of individual victories and team victories.

Toolkit

To bring out the best in our people, we set clear deliverables and job expectations. We assess their IQ, EQ and CQ profiles in a supportive system that promotes mental fitness.

To build your people up:

- Design your organisational reporting structure and job roles diligently to meet business goals. You must know what you need from each role, and whether the people in those roles have the right skills.

- When hiring new staff, make sure you recruit the right person.

- Never promote people to take on legislative and cultural accountability when they can't do it.

- Choose your step-ups carefully and train them in basic leadership and Safe Systems of Work.

- Give them a good coach and get them to prove their worth. Remove those who do not meet expectations.

- Train your people using the best trainers. Assess demonstrated activity, not paper qualifications, to see if it's working.

- Hold people accountable to the business plan.

- Do not overglorify success. Just doing your job does not warrant a bonus.

- Set comfortable stretch targets and then celebrate once they are achieved.

- Thank your people for doing a great job.

Insights

If you want Link and Flow to abound you must feed it with the right type of skill and it will soon lead you to Grow. Promoting a technically proficient person with little or no demonstrated leadership and assertiveness skills is a recipe for disaster and needs to be avoided.

If you want a high-performance team, create a mentally fit environment. If something challenging happens, an effective manager should know how to help their team maintain optimum functioning.

The most satisfying part of putting in the effort to be a hands-on manager and building people up is being rewarded by their great work.

A few years ago, a friend of mine (Kris's) who works for a major insurer suggested that when a worker has a workers compensation incident and is beginning the process, the first question you should ask them is, 'Do you like the company you work in?'

I thought it was a pretty odd question to prioritise. I could think of many other questions that would be racing through my mind. What if they were injured and needed first aid?

My wise friend remarked that if the person loved their workplace, they came back to work a lot quicker than if they hated the company.

This really highlights why a mentally fit culture needs to be in a business before incidents happen. If you wait to do something till after the incident, it is too late and will cost the business dearly.

If you, as a manager, can create a workplace that supports and benefits your workers, they will be better engaged. The more they trust and believe that the company has their interests at heart, the more they can overcome obstacles and perform at their best.

Managers can do a lot to instil that trust.

Without great performers you get pretty poor Link and even poorer Flow in your business. You need people who can and will make the difference, because when they do your business will grow, your culture will shine, people will know what is expected and how, and staff will stay around.

Never lower your recruitment standards because when you let a zombie-like infection into your workplace, you know what is going to happen.

My Mental Fitness Checklist

- Identify the stars in your teams. Create a plan to build their future leadership skills. Can you provide a 12-month program?

- Identify the skills your Frontliners and Managers are lacking. Create a plan to address this.

- Assess your org and job designs. Do they identify the strengths and skills necessary to succeed?

- List the ways you hold your people accountable for results.

Chapter 17

Messing up big time takes seconds

This story is about how damaging first impressions can wipe out your influence. The mental fitness tools we used focus on being genuine and aligning what we say with what we truly believe. The insights we learned were that EQ exercises can improve mental fitness.

Story: Outback jerk

I (Kris) was at a remote work site in the Australian outback. There's nothing cuddly or 'feel good' out there amidst the dust and extreme heat. Yet, how managers and workers feel about each other is critical to the bottom line.

When we meet someone for the first time, we decide within 30 seconds whether we trust and respect them. This is critical for managers of large work teams.

Harvard researcher and psychologist Amy Cuddy suggests that how much your workers *respect* you depends on your competence. You might think competence is the most important thing in a work context but it isn't. How much they *trust* you is more important than respect. Trust is based on the warmth of your personality.

When it comes to work performance, trust has more influence than respect. For teams to succeed, there needs to be genuine trust and respect, both ways, between managers and workers.

As the site manager showed me around and introduced me to the teams, a live situation unfolded to illustrate this point.

We were walking through the workshop area when we came across a manager talking loudly to 20 welders and boilermakers. The manager had his hands on his hips and occasionally gesticulated to emphasise his point.

Even before I could make out what the manager was saying, my 'low mental fitness' detector was activated. The workers were looking down, arms crossed. They were disengaged. Some looked fed up.

As I drew closer, the manager's words made me shake my head.

'This should not have happened. Who f*cking ...'

The manager was new and not an experienced workshop member. This was his first talk to the group, and he had gone in too gung-ho and unknowingly flushed whatever trust and respect was present in the group down the toilet.

Afterwards, I pulled him aside and asked him to consider the impact of his statement and its delivery.

One month later, I spoke with the manager again. He saw what difficulty he had caused for himself by the way he addressed his staff for the first time.

Toolkit

It took that manager more than six months to repair the damage and bring the group's mental fitness level back where it was. We mentored him to exercise trust and respect in the way he interacted with key influencers and individuals reporting to him, and in so doing build up the trust and respect they had of him. This raised their CQ enough for them to work together successfully with strong workplace mental fitness.

If you and I were playing golf and I started to criticise your game and strategies from the first hole, you'd probably be off your game within a short period of time. As a matter of fact, it would be amazing if you lasted 18 holes with me without either getting angry or refusing to play with me.

If the same thing happens at work, subordinates may not speak up, but they do get sick of it. So let's look at what we can do to stop messing things up.

To communicate effectively as a mentally fit manager:

- Hold everyone, including your leadership, accountable to your communication policies. Survey your workforce and ask them how good the communication is.

- Follow up wherever you have registered an issue; don't let it fester.

- Use a continuous improvement approach at the team level. Respect it and follow up.

- Keep people informed, even when there is nothing to say, because they will think you are holding back. Consider starting a continuous improvement committee made up from teams.

- Review the org design carefully as the signs will be there. Don't wait too long as some damage can be irreparable.

- Use an IOC so you can stay on top of the structure.

Insights

The mentally unfit manager did not intend to alienate his team. In some circles the leader leads by displaying aggression and domination, by whipping their team into shape.

Not in today's world, you don't.

Aggression can destroy anyone's influence as a leader in 30 seconds. EQ matters. Help aggressive managers realise how much damage they are causing, but without blaming or shaming. Highlight what both of you want to achieve; condemn the action, not the person.

The manager learnt that bossing people around was not the same as being an effective leader. A good leader shows humility and acknowledges their team members as professionals in their field. A manager's job is to get the best out of them.

To be an effective leader today, you cannot merely pay lip service to mental fitness. To build mental fitness in our teams, we have to start with ourselves. Be the catalyst for establishing an environment of trust and respect. Then, success can be a regular part of the business dynamic.

Remember that everyone at work contributes to the wellbeing of the culture, that's *everyone*, so have a strategy of inclusion; be seen walking around and saying hello. Ask people for their opinions and don't be afraid to discuss what is practicable with people to hear their perspectives.

It is much easier to sustain a good workplace culture than it is to be continually fighting fires and dealing with stress. Make the connection between changing your culture, and getting better safety behaviour and productivity outcomes.

My Mental Fitness Checklist

- Rate how aware you are of your own feelings and others' feelings, and how well you manage your own feelings and others' feelings. Consider making an action plan for your own development.

- Rate the EQ of your team members. Do the EQ scores suggest the team is high-performing? Make an action plan for everyone to participate in EQ-boosting activities.

- Openly discuss the cultural environment with your leadership team and set expectations.

Chapter 18

Say no to being a 'Yes' person

This story cautions that being a 'yes' person can lead to career suicide. The mental fitness tool to use is to exercise the courage to rock the boat if you need to do so. The insights learned are that saying yes is not always best for the business.

Story: People pleasers and bullies are a perfect match

A very promising junior manager I (Kris) know was ecstatic to be promoted to CFO. Can you picture a Cheshire cat grinning? That was her.

As a senior manager, Jennifer had many more opportunities to influence and change the business she was in.

I said to her, 'Promise me one thing. Don't say "yes".'

Her response was a snort of derision and a chuckle of, 'Don't worry about me, mate.'

Jennifer went on to enthusiastically agree with every opinion the CEO expressed. Perhaps it was her inexperience that led to over-cooperating. This meant she was not exercising leadership and independent initiative in her senior role.

The carnage that ensued was as spectacular as it was nasty. A rookie with so much talent fell off the throne, lost her crown, and was mercilessly destroyed by the business. The culture of distrust and disrespect set up an 'us vs them' mindset that would take years to be removed from that business.

While some people may be voluntary 'yes' men, coerced 'yes' men exist as well. I know a coerced yes man who endured months and months of stress, harassment and bullying. One day he just broke down and cried and never returned to work.

Surely you would think a workplace could see this happening, so why let it happen? There has to be something dreadfully wrong with the culture if cases like this happen. How many more cases must be festering unseen?

There will never be any Flow of optimum value where people feel that they can't contribute. Whether it is a lack of assertiveness in some staff or a widespread issue in the workplace, it cannot be allowed to continue.

As managers, we have the duty of care to build workplace mental fitness. We must do our best to ensure that our people are not traumatised at work.

Toolkit

Succession failure could have been prevented in this case by clarifying the key deliverables of the role to someone new to a senior position, an experienced senior manager mentoring her, and providing a robust induction program.

To be successful, or help someone do so:

- Survey employees and leadership and find where over-cooperation exists.

- Make a stand to say what is right, not what you think the big boss wants to hear.

- Recognise that the manager who needs to always hear 'yes' is setting up the junior colleague for failure.

- Induct promotees to the technical IQ, managerial EQ and collaborative CQ needed to perform well at their new level of responsibility.

- Learn the art of self-review before applying principles to your staff.

- Humility is a very important skill. Develop self to develop others.

To help someone who feels forced to agree with the way higher-ups want things done:

- Check if lack of assertiveness is an issue and take action to close the gap.

- Reflect on the Toolkit from chapter 16 for building your people up and ensure these are implemented in your organisation.

- Identify an employee assistance program and suggest it to your workforce.

- Create opportunities for people to talk over their issues at work.

- Make your leadership empathetic towards people who struggle so they have an avenue of support.

- Review how effectively your workplace handles bullying and harassment.

Insights

If the organisation demands blind loyalty then the management are in a bind.

Many of us have seen 'yes' people in action. Sometimes the workplace is ruled by micromanagers and procrastinators with cold and clinical approaches. The demands these people make are sometimes too strong to be contested by the weak, or so relentless that it is just easier not to fight it. There is a lack of mental fitness here.

Sometimes emotional bulldozers like to have people they can manipulate as this makes them look good in the eyes of their managers, but it does little for the mental wellbeing of anyone copping or witnessing the bullying. Many war stories are probably whispered in canteens and lunch messes, accompanied by stressful sleepless nights.

My Mental Fitness Checklist

- The next time you catch yourself saying 'yes', check your motivation behind it.

- Brainstorm instances when saying 'no' is a sign of effective leadership.

- Define the difference between being a 'yes' person and being cooperative.

- Evaluate your leadership team. Who has too much aggression?

- Check your IOC for any imbalances in communication making it difficult to get a two-way flow of understanding.

Chapter 19
The brilliant destroyer

This story is about the two models of destroyers you should get rid of. The tools we used were to build your emotional and collaborative quotients (EQ and CQ). The insights we gained were to not be a 'competent asshole'.

Story: The dark side of competitive achievers

Imagine letting a hippo loose in a supermarket.

You got that? Well, Gareth, a ruthless and powerful superintendent, was the management equivalent of that hippo.

He was hungry for promotion and demanded total compliance and no mistakes. He could see himself at the next level as a divisional manager, or even higher, so he worked relentlessly on his promotability but was absolutely blind to the damage he was doing to his team. Hence 'brilliant destroyer'.

Every morning, he was highly critical of something. Anyone who walked by his office could expect to hear him in there giving someone a dressing down.

A blind hippo in a china shop. No bull.

Once he started receiving coaching, his eyes were prised wide open. He realised he was in a downward spiral. The people he was leading didn't like him at all, and his employability was only as good as his relationships with them.

Over several months, he exercised the courage to deflate his ego and apologised to his team for his arrogant behaviour. He then set about building a relationship that valued their input.

The hippo no longer treated his people like dogs. The destroyer turned things around before he destroyed himself.

Destroyers come in many guises, some seemingly respectable. Be on the alert. Let's give you another example.

Erica did all the right things. She studied hard, made it to university, graduated with excellent grades, and worked for the best companies. She fought her way up several rungs of the corporate ladder from junior manager to general manager. Collateral damage in the form of alienated peers and intimidated subordinates was to be expected — too bad.

Isn't this supposed to be the classic high achiever with the meteoric career? Just look at her impressive LinkedIn profile! Well, yes, if you want to be a good performer. But no, if you want to be a great leader.

We see this pattern all too often in ambitious managers, including ourselves. When society endorses competitiveness more than cooperation, it becomes acceptable that being a winner means making everyone else a loser. In a dog-eat-dog world, it's okay to be a bitch.

I (Kris) woke up when I hit the ceiling of output: my team still waited for me to tell them what to do. 500 functional people waiting for me to tell them what to do is 500 too many.

If I didn't crack the whip, the workplace became a circus.

It was sobering to realise that as a manager I had not created anything valuable beyond myself. Instead, I was destroying the expression of others' full potential to fuel my own ascension. I was hit hard that even if people thought of me as a skilled individual, I was a failure as a manager. It took too much energy to achieve success every day.

If I were a true star, I would be able to bring out my staff's brilliance effortlessly.

You'll grow old very lonely, if you think you can succeed in life without uplifting people. You may have very high standards and feel that others just don't meet them.

Well, good luck. I hope you have heating in your ivory tower.

Toolkit

Too often, companies retain and promote brilliant destroyers. You've probably met a few in your work life. Our consulting work often involves spotting, mentoring or removing these people from an organisation in trouble.

To attract talent that lights up your whole organisation:

- Build a champion team, not a team of champions. How often do we see star players who can't work together?

- Build trust and respect with connection and understanding. Managers who achieve this are worth their weight in gold. Promote off the floor, yes, and train them into the role.

- Be careful while using psychometric testing that you don't filter out diversity and cultural difference — this is essential to combat groupthink and maximise team potential.

- Put a focus on life experience along with other traditional measures of intelligence.

- Remember failure is a critical part of learning.

- Use resumes as guidance, not the Bible.

If you recognise yourself as a brilliant destroyer, consider the following career stretches:

- Understand that you alone are not the answer to business success.

- Be humble. You don't need to become a wimp, but you do need to see and say how your behaviour has not been in the best interests of team development.

- Understand that any legacy you leave behind will always come back to haunt you—your cold and clinical approach might fit at a very high level, but it will never be accepted at the workplace.

- Approach the team with empathy. See some situations as a chance to work together to get a solution.

- Do not tolerate poor behaviour, but adopt a coaching style that builds people up, and doesn't break them down.

- Use engagement strategies when you communicate, don't just destroy character.

- Get people to want to come to your office.

- Have an open-door policy.

- Create opportunity.

- Build mental fitness.

Insights

The brilliant destroyer will ruin everything, they are so good at it. They only see one direction and use everyone and everything as collateral to get them there.

You can ever only be as good as the team and the legacy you leave behind. When everyone hates being around you your career will suffer—there is absolutely no doubt about that.

Companies that keep brilliant destroyers forget that their individual high performance comes at the price of low performance and morale in the people and teams they supervise.

In startup adviser and psychiatry professor Dr Cameron Sepah's universe, this 'Competent Asshole' gets only 50 out of 100 points (where 100 points is optimal performance).[24] Competent Nice Guys/Gals score 75 points and Outstanding Nice Guys/Gals get 100 points.

Put a high-impact leader in place and the fun begins. Just last week, a freshly appointed Driver won $10 million in new contracts for an industrial client after swooping in and sweeping out old habits and attitudes. He did a brilliant job as the proverbial new broom.

Yes, it's easier to ponder what Dr Sepah calls the 'No Asshole Rule' than to practise it. A leader who makes every single team member a star is the true creator, so we urge you to do what you can to destroy any brilliant destroyers you may have in your organisation.

My Mental Fitness Checklist

- Identify the brilliant destroyers in your organisation. Trace their impact. What needs to happen to reduce the impact of Assholes, and increase the influence of Nice Guys/Gals?

- Success does not always manifest itself in qualifications. Where else do your people need to succeed?

- List what you would do differently if you had the chance to do it all over again.

- Identify some of the best things your teams have done to make you look good, and list some ways you might make that happen more often.

Chapter 20

Living on a roller coaster

This story is about how unmanaged personal stress can destroy a manager's workplace effectiveness. The mental fitness tools are to build resilience and balance. The insights are that a mentally fit approach to your staff's personal issues can prevent them from becoming workplace issues.

Story: It's not strictly personal when it affects the business

They say 'don't bring your work home'. But what if 'home' follows you to work?

Annie had a terrific job where she was paid very well for her bookkeeping skills. As a single mum, she appreciated being allowed to work within school hours (typically 8.30 am to 3 pm) and have every second Saturday off in the busy season.

Being newly divorced, she was still struggling to manage the issues she had with her ex-husband, and was estranged from her teenage daughter. She was passive and introverted in her approach to problems, and so hadn't resolved them very well.

Things became awkward at work when Annie started to bring her personal problems to work and dumping them on anyone close enough to listen. They were sympathetic at first, but soon her erratic lack of control over her moods started to bring them down. They started to avoid her. It was destroying the cohesion and culture of her team.

Annie was in no state to realise her negative impact at work. Her personal and team productivity plummeted. People were unhappy. Not only was she putting her livelihood in jeopardy, she could lose the respect of her peers and her financial stability.

A mentally fit organisation would not allow this situation to occur. On a smaller scale, if there was mental fitness at team level, the team may well have fixed the issue themselves and not allowed it to get worse.

In this case, the situation had been allowed to fester so much that the easy way out was to make the person redundant because the business had no other way of dealing with the issue. The job was contracted out.

There is a clear lesson here about mental health and its impact on daily issues. If there is organisational mental fitness, everyone involved is empowered to handle the issue without affecting their work, and the person in question is referred to professional services.

Most business owners and directors would agree with Tony Hsieh, the CEO of Zappos.com, that, 'If you get the culture right, most of the other stuff will just take care of itself.' However, most business leaders don't know where to start.

Well, we do.

Emotional roller coasters can be awkward and embarrassing to deal with, but if you let them run away unchecked they could derail your workforce from focusing on work.

With a plan in place and your ear on the ground, you can be more successful in spotting roller coasters as they start, and not allow them to gather momentum and sweep everyone else off for the ride.

Strong empathetic leadership controls the roller coaster, so understand that you have a responsibility to deal with discomfort at all staff levels, and mind your own response too.

Toolkit

It is our responsibility as managers to see to our staff's collective wellbeing and any distraught staff member's wellbeing. It's not a matter of being nice. It's a matter of being keeping the workplace functional even when faced by challenges with emotional origins.

To see to your staff's collective wellbeing:

- Start talking with your staff generically about this issue.

- Have an open-door policy for people to relate problems and issues that may affect their work.

- Make your staff aware they do not have to carry the burden of these issues.

- Engage monthly with your staff to emphasise that you are there to support them to be successful focusing on achieving what they need at work, and if the roller coaster is still affecting them, issues can be talked through.

- Seriously consider a mental fitness program, especially in a small business where one person's issues can affect the whole team.

To see to the wellbeing of the person generating the roller coaster:

- Acknowledge that they are in an emotionally trying state, and get the message across that you are there to support them being successful at work despite what they are going through.

- Remember your role as manager is to support them being successful at work, and not to play psychologist and directly support them to deal with their emotional roller coaster.

- Provide employee assistance program options that are practicable for your business. Suggest ways they could seek help to manage their stress and, if you have the skills, mentor them to self-soothe and maintain a peak performance state.

- If, despite your best efforts to support their wellbeing, they still cannot fulfil their duties, then look at managing their exit.

- When someone is in an upset state, they may become irritable with others. Do not let their state be an excuse for condoning bullying, harassment or unprofessional communication at the workplace. To be proactive, step up training on positive interactive behaviours and how to deal with harassment.

Insights

While it is not your responsibility as a manager to resolve your workers' emotional issues, deal with personal emotional issues, or treat mental health, it *is* your responsibility to support the wellbeing of your staff so they can be successful in their work role.

If you respond to this situation in a mentally unfit manner, it increases their personal distress and reduces their capacity to fulfil their work role, and can also affects their colleagues' personal distress and work capacity.

So there are real reasons why you need to deal with this in a timely and effective manner.

Living on the roller coaster is not just for the person whose issues are being brought to work. It also stresses co-workers and management and, if left unresolved, creates embarrassment and dislocation in the team, which in turn can affect productivity and efficiency and may even lead to increased incidents.

My Mental Fitness Checklist

- Observe work interactions among your staff for a week and take note of what it says about your workplace culture. What values are being expressed through action?

- Map the areas of workplace culture you want to improve, and start researching ways to achieve them with a mentally fit approach.

- Devise a strategy for spotting and stopping roller coasters in their tracks.

- Assess whether there is enough assertiveness in your workplace culture to deal with the issues at work. If not, what is your plan to deal with it?

Chapter 21

The rise and rise of the meat robot

This story is about how perception is reality. The tools we used were to respect everyone's self worth regardless of their net worth. The insight we gained was that putting people first can be great for business.

Story: Treat humans humanely

When are we going to stop treating workers like meat robots? They are human beings!

More than once, we've come out of meetings with lawyers on workers compensation cases angry and disheartened. They cared more about how much it would cost the client in workers compensation than the wellbeing of the injured party.

In one case, Adam was a master welder in his home country who'd just arrived to work in an Australian city. The new work environment was a large fabrication plant with 200 employees. He was in an unfamiliar environment and spoke no English. Yes, they had hired an interpreter, but she was only available 9 to 5.

He was on night shift working on a massive steel girder and his supervisor had said, 'Keep us updated and if you're unsure then seek us out', but of course he didn't understand.

Half an hour before his 12-hour shift ended, the steel girder fell and crushed his arms — and his award-studded welding career along with it.

The insurer was worried. The workers compensation could get expensive.

The lawyers on both sides feigned interest in cost to the company and the injured party, while their minds crunched through the fees they could charge. A mildly hypocritical stance in our opinion. No concern for psychosocial harm. We certainly hope things change into the future.

In another case, Bruce was a road train truck driver. He regularly drove 14- to 16-hour shifts transporting refrigerated foods across thousands of kilometres and was too familiar with the endless landscape of the Australian outback. He was often away from home for days on end, having to make a 72-hour turnaround for deliveries to the eastern states and back to Western Australia.

This was his third claim in as many years for a bad back made worse by long hours sitting in one position. But this time, he was claiming for mental stress as well, as his wife wanted to divorce him because she could not deal anymore with his chronic depression (which came from feeling helpless due to widespread incompetence at work and his back problems).

The HR department was worried. The workers compensation could get expensive.

You see it everywhere: jobs and work hours designed to maximise profits with minimal consideration for the toll it takes on the worker's physical and mental health. Workers who cannot handle 15-hour shifts? Replace them. Let those who can and want the job do the work.

Is it in anyone's best interest to treat these workers like meat robots?

We regularly talk with Davo, a shiftworker from a mentally unfit workplace. In recent times he has become angrier and more frustrated with his fellow workers because they do not pull their weight and do their share of the work. What is the leadership doing when it takes peer-to-peer bullying to get work done?

Surely there is a manual somewhere in Davo's workplace that clearly states standard operating procedures. But with little or no mental fitness leadership taking charge, even the most competent workers turn feral and wreck their self-leadership. Whether you hire incompetence, nice people or just put bums on seats, it's all the same. The business suffers because people either cannot or will not be high-performing over long periods of time without proper leadership and supervision. You should not be surprised when this creates chaos.

Toolkit

To combat a workplace that treats its people like meat robots, all policies and procedures must be reviewed with mental fitness in mind.

The mentally fit organisations we helped create have achieved spectacular business success, such as a 400 per cent increase in revenue, and a 90 per cent decrease in safety incidents. Yes, this shows that putting people first can profit the business.

To build a successful business where both profits and people thrive:

- Decrease the number of forms and procedures.
- Improve communication in the organisation. Everyone must feel empowered to have a voice.
- Ensure use of casual labour is not a revolving door.

- Ensure the value of each role is clear, and linked to business goals.
- Train management to manage the unique individual not the 'average' worker.

Insights

We're not against progress, but we need to be careful of how we define it. Let's look a little deeper and see the individual humans in these roles.

Let's not just patch up the human fallout from the way work is currently organised, but review, rethink and redesign these very work systems instead.

When will we realise that if we treat people like meat robots, we are creating financial gain at the expense of human losses such as injuries, poor productivity, disengagement and burnout?

We really need to see that it's the people who create the company's wealth. It is their actions or omissions that lead us into chaos or profit.

If management distrusts its workers and assumes that they are always trying to get workers comp to get out of having to work, it will result in self-fulfilling prophecies.

Let's treat every worker like a human, not a meat robot. If you are paying a much higher than industry average premium for workers comp or damage insurance, then you should consider how much you would save over five years if you create a mentally fit work environment. People need to feel recognised and valued: that's all you need to do. Create an environment where people matter. You get a lot more out of them than a meat robot.

My Mental Fitness Checklist

- Have a procedure and form review meeting to assess mental fitness impact.

- Present a live interactive org chart at every board meeting to see all levels of the business and view the vitals.

- How could you change things at work so that people matter and work flows?

- Consider some sort of career progression program or incentives for people to contribute at a higher level.

Chapter 22

Habits can change

This story is about Graeme's happy reinvention. The tools we used were raining, not blaming. The insights we gained are that managers create winners with mentoring. Be open to change; there's always hope.

Story: Passing the buck

A crane operator was perched in his cabin, 30 storeys up, and was moving concrete slabs when his crane broke free from its support structure. It keeled over and crashed into a skyscraper, trapping the operator inside.

Miraculously, he survived with only a broken arm. Six workers on the ground escaped with minor injuries, and the damage and delay to the project exceeded $200 000.

Graeme, the site manager, launched an investigation. The finger of blame was pointed at Barry, the supervisor. Investigations revealed that Barry saw everything and had signed off on the lift study without really understanding the job. He said nothing about his process and did nothing to reduce safety risks. Damningly, he had initially lied that he was not there at the time.

Graeme let Barry completely carry the can for the safety breach.

Our investigation of the events leading up to the incident showed that Barry had exercised poor supervision of his team and their activities. Low mental fitness hijacked the day, and we're not only talking about Barry.

Barry was the product of four years under Graeme's leadership.

It was obvious he had not been taught the right practices, and had not been held accountable in the past. He became complacent when previous breaches didn't result in safety incidents.

The organisation never formed the safety habit. It was an accident waiting to happen.

No-one was going to change the status quo. There was too much social risk of rocking the boat to doing things differently, even if that was the right thing to do.

Like the holes in consecutive slices of Swiss cheese, the events lined up and the crane driver incident spilt the beans on what was really going on before the incident.

A whole heap of 'at risk' behaviours had gone unchecked for too long, and the number of near misses piled up, ignored or unnoticed, breeding complacency.

The cause of the accident is not a mystery: low mental fitness.

Of all the incidents I (Kris) have investigated, I am still yet to find one that is a true mystery. The ability to foresee the future becomes quite relevant in safety. A lack of incidents becomes a representation of mental fitness. We cannot get to zero incidents but we can do so much better than now. You have to keep a finger on the pulse of these things. And you can, with the IOC.

You see, a fatality is not a matter of bad luck. Mentally fit managers create their own luck because luck favours the prepared.

For over a year, I worked with Graeme to get him to see that his laid-back, low people and low task focus was the opposite of the mental fitness focus and leadership impact we're looking for.

Graeme was the classic 'pass mark' manager who did nothing to nurture his team or advance his own professional growth.

It may have served him in the short term but did nothing to establish effective workplace relationships or lead team effectiveness. His credibility was seriously damaged and no-one respected his 'leadershit'. Senior management got wind of it and moved him to a new site.

That was Graeme's second chance.

He worked very hard to turn his profile around. He changed his leadership style and practised a high task, high people approach.

Everyone who knew what he was like at the old site was amazed at the change. He started to build respect and credibility amongst his team. Graeme became mentally fit.

He gets it now and knows the realm of high touch is as important as high concept. His new supervisor, Brad, likes working under him and together they lead the team and get the results that a continuous improvement model requires.

Some people can make amazing changes to the way they do things but changing habits that have taken years to develop can be very difficult for many, especially when no-one is holding them accountable for their poor performance.

Why would people want to change anyway, especially when they are treated poorly or have no personal reason to do so? The team is as good as its leader and the leader is as good as its manager, and so on. When there are silos of operation where one department is disconnected from another, you see the different standards with varying degrees of mental fitness, many with none.

Toolkit

All too often we blame the team (the buggers didn't follow the plan and now we have to do it all again!). Habits can change when people are held accountable (especially the leaders). People are doomed to make mistakes, but it's how many, and how severe they are, that determines their life in the team. If you do not enforce any standards then you can't expect to get them, so here are some good tips on how to facilitate change for the better:

- Understand that shit happens for a reason.

- Know that decisive leadership can prevent the team from straying, incident rates from increasing and equipment damage from escalating.

- Identify the real requirements of effective leadership at the supervision level and get it. Take no prisoners.

- Get your supervisors communicating the new practice to the teams.

- Implement a set of non-negotiables, enforce them and build new standards.

- Coach and mentor your employees until they get it. Change the ones who can't or won't.

- Implement a continuous improvement program, so people have a say in how the place is run. Maybe even sponsor a monthly prize for those who have shown true grit.

- Create opportunities to participate, transfer to other departments or offer flexibility options; they will all get great results.

- Show them you care. We know that can be tough but if you want the results, walk your talk.

Insights

There is everything to be gained where opportunity, acceptance and mattering live. Funny — that just sounds like mental fitness.

People can and will change where the environment fosters it. Leave people to their own devices for too long and they will lose the motivation to do it your way. Be on the alert for anyone who feels helpless or hopeless, and help them get out of it. So, this suggests the ball is in your court and will stay there. It's how you play the game that makes the difference.

My Mental Fitness Checklist

- Identify how many mentally unfit leadership profiles are in your organisation.

- If you have them, identify the strategies you can use to fix the problem.

- Create a list of what you can do to invigorate the team.

- Create and communicate high enough expectations on your leaders to foster and facilitate change.

- Consider some small incentive schemes that will help people to change.

- Implement career talks and succession planning — it might just get some people up and motivated to excel.

Chapter 23
The one-sided coin

This story is about what happens when procedures get put before people. The tools we used were about understanding workers' workspace. The insights we gained were that it's important to take a walk in your workers' shoes.

Story: Blue-sky thinking in white-collar offices

Lawyers' offices have breathtaking views. Shiny glass and steel, jarrah and leather. They sit amidst blue skies and pristine white clouds, looming over lesser buildings and the hum of CBD traffic.

In one such office I (Kris) was chatting with a couple of Armani-clad lawyers.

'If a worker has an accident at work, it is usually his fault and the company is not liable,' Armani 1 said.

'The SSoW (Safe System of Work) has already assessed the risk of his work. They've identified the hazards, and trained him to deal with work risks. When the employee stuffs up, it's tragic. But it's not the company's fault,' said Armani 2.

I piped up. 'How is that right? If there are a lot of safety incidents, obviously the SSoW has failed. It's the management's responsibility to provide duty of care. An organisation that displays low mental fitness for work is not fulfilling their duty of care.'

'Yes they are,' replied Armani 1. 'There's an SSoW. If something does go wrong, then the individual didn't follow procedure.'

'As long as we have a plan for them, they won't hurt themselves,' said Armani 2 confidently. 'They know their job so nothing will go wrong.'

That's the blue-sky thinking in white-collar offices that screws blue-collar workers over twice.

It makes logical sense to the analytical left brains of these smartly suited and scented professionals who have no idea what the blue-collar worker deals with in their everyday work.

The daily challenge of working in a high-risk environment with multiple risk factors takes a significant toll on these workers' mental fitness for duty.

The more safety incidents or even near misses occur, the more they show up the SSoW as a work of fantasy. It is not recognising the real problem or doing anything effective to get rid of it.

The lawyers see the situation from the perspective of their lofty corporate office in the sky, which is only one side of the coin.

That office environment is a far cry from what your truck driver, bus driver, welder or labourer copes with on a daily basis: high stress, high fatigue, remote isolation, boredom and tedium, and helplessness due to having low authority and earning minimum wage all the while.

These workers are crying out silently through the statistics: billions of dollars lost every year due to poor mental health and wellbeing (see the figures shared in the preface).

They deserve a lot better.

Toolkit

A continual improvement program will often result in much safer and more effective ways of doing the job.

To create a two-sided coin:

- Ensure supervisors assess risks with workers' field input. Investigate the root cause of why things go wrong at the team level and you will find cultural and organisational factors play a leading role.

- Demand that managers stop hiding behind ineffective SSoWs and provide more than armchair leadership.

- Ensure effective risk assessments by auditing every high-risk job and holding whoever signed off the risk assessment responsible.

- Create engagement—that's a two-way thing where both sides are equal.

- Create Link and Flow.

- Hold every manager responsible for the incidents and damage caused at team level, no matter how busy they are.

- Review your Managing 'In' Design.

- Make your not-negotiables not negotiable to every level.

- Take stock of the pain this causes and seek solutions, but your not-negotiables are for the whole team.

- Believe in your people. It might be hard early on but when the power of mental fitness kicks in you will be glad you did.

Insights

One-sided coins cannot buy health. Neither side of the coin is better or worse. Only two-sided coins have real value.

We use universities to tell white-collar management more and more about what they should do for blue-collar employees.

The other side of the coin is to understand our workers' reality so we can be managers and leaders who can handle the truth. We need to look from the inside out and not the outside in.

Get the perspective from those who do the job. Take a walk in their shoes. How else can you truly appreciate what working 12 hours straight in steel-capped boots at the mercy of the weather or in windowless confined spaces feels like? What they say and how they do the job can create significant inroads into understanding how it needs to be done. And, guess what? You will have listened to them. Amazing.

My Mental Fitness Checklist

- Recall any commendable actions or mistakes made by your workers. Are their managers held responsible for them?

- Review your list of non-negotiable work behaviours. In practice, do they apply to managers and supervisors as well as workers?

- Do the actions and beliefs of your supervisors demonstrate that they are true ambassadors and implementers of your Safe System of Work?

- List your recruitment strategies. Evaluate if each one sets you up for success or failure in the workplace.

Chapter 24
A key to spectacular success

This story is about not letting your Achilles heel stop you from dancing. The tools we used were performance management and mentoring. The insights we gained were the wisdom of not giving a f*ck, and that there is no end point to people development.

Story: Not calling 'timber!' when failure occurs

Many years ago, when the native timber industry was closed, a few hundred workers suddenly found themselves out of work. To them, it must have felt like someone calling 'timber!' after cutting down the tree of their livelihood.

John's job was to help them find new jobs.

Having only ever worked in the timber industry, the workers never considered that they had transferable skills that could be used elsewhere. We mentored them for successful job transitions, and connected them to new roles that valued their skills.

What looks like failure can be the seed of success in new pastures.

A few years ago, I (Kris) made it to the final interview with an exciting new global food and beverage brand coming to Australia. Everything was going great and the role was surely mine.

Till I got to the very last step — psychometric testing. Aarrggghhh!!

Abstract reasoning annoyed me. I'd never understood why X is to Y like 'plate' is to 'kitten' … what?!

To cut a long story short, I failed spectacularly. When the recruitment guy rang to break the news, I could almost hear his 'wow, that was ugly' tone over the phone.

Fast forward to today and hey! Last week I actually paid a princely sum to get some psychometric testing done as part of a career development application. I scored an amazing 94 per cent! Never say never!

I've been making friends with 'abstract reasoning' after transferring it from my Failure bucket to my Work Improvement bucket (refer to figure 6.2 in chapter 6).

Of course everyone fails sometimes in something or other, so failure is not something to be worried or upset about; leaving the failure item in the Failure bucket and not doing anything about it is.

Happily, items in the Work Improvement bucket can lead to new Success outcomes.

So, allow yourself and others to fail, then empty the Failure bucket.

Mick was someone allowed to fail. As a supervisor, he was great on most days, but had a temper that flared up on occasion. This rattled his team and eroded their trust in and respect for him.

Mick was aware of his shortcoming and keen to change. However, being keen and actually changing are two different things.

The mind is like an engine. If cared for and serviced regularly, it works well for a long time. In Mick's case, his mental fitness toolkit was lacking the tools for servicing the anger component.

In Barbara's case, she was lacking other tools.

Barbara was unwittingly set up to fail. She was promoted to manager level with very little exposure to that level of leadership. Yes, she had been a hands-on supervisor for some time, but no, she had no formal managerial training at all.

To say she was under-equipped to do the job was an understatement. Her company knew that but promoted her anyway. This happens more than you think. Her Achilles heel was her lack of assertiveness. That limited her communication and people management. She was hungry for someone to teach her how.

Toolkit

So how did we add tools to Mick and Barbara's mental fitness kits?

In Mick's case, the first step was to acknowledge that getting angry is an understandable reaction to some triggers.

The second step is harder. How do we help him self-manage anger? Mick worked really hard with his in-field coach, John, to work on his mental fitness challenge without taking things out on his team. Mick's aggressive tendency remains a work area for him and he is allowed to continue to try even if he fails. In this way he chips away at the degree of failure and minimises it over time.

In Barbara's case, breaking her old habits was the hardest thing.

If criticised, she would get all bent out of shape, and make excuses for why things were not followed up. Two years of mentoring and training workshops later, Barbara has grown in confidence and professionalism. Our mentally fit approach prevented her from burning out, and ongoing support can only help her become an even better manager. Left to her own devices, she would never have made it this far.

We must help the Micks and Barbaras win because it does a lot to help them build mental fitness, self-leadership, self-esteem and confidence. This can make a considerable difference to their lives. We've had spouses of people we are mentoring say, 'I don't know what you've done to my better half, but they are now excited about their future.' A little bit goes a long way. It makes us so proud.

The satisfaction we derive from developing our people is both personal and professional. Imagine how phenomenal a high-performance team you could build if you replicated this mentally fit approach to people management across your workforce.

To develop your people so they are not continually failing:

- Expect that people will make some mistakes—you do too. Some people are really good at some things and hopeless at others. Drip-feed regular mentoring and coaching, it's not a once-off thing. Let mistakes bring education, not punishment.

- Keep people positive, even when they have stuffed it up. Treat people with respect and help them not get bent out of shape when things go wrong. Instead, help them focus on taking accountable action to make things right.

- Get Job Design right. Look for the people with the right skills set or train them to build up their capabilities.

- The journey of assertiveness is critical to many during a learning pathway, so make sure you understand what they have to offer and what level they need to achieve to be good in the role.

- Create a mattering climate where people know that help is right next door if they need it. Give constant feedback on progress.

- Have your senior leaders learn how to coach. If you put someone in a role, then you are responsible for them. Help them to succeed by giving them the support they need.

- Understand that you cannot get Flow to happen around incompetence and ignorance.

- Be patient; some will take time to master the concepts, especially if you threw them into the deep end. Communicate often with those who are learning as they need constant feedback and validation.

Insights

Failing spectacularly is part of the road to success and part of workplace mental fitness.

In Japan, broken pottery is often repaired with lacquer mixed with gold or other precious metals. It's called *kintsugi* or 'golden joinery'. The flaw is seen as a unique piece of the object's history, which adds to its beauty. Consider this when you feel broken. Consider your management technique and how you cope with personal and team member failure.

We know it's hard: when you are really strong at something, and you see someone really weak at something, you really want to rush right in and tell them how it's done *already*.

Holding back and letting someone experience their own learning process can be painful at times.

We recommend the perfect book for letting the Micks in your life own their struggle. In the words of Mark Manson, who wrote the book on *The Subtle Art of Not Giving a F*ck*,[25] it is not about being indifferent, but about not giving 'a f*ck about adversity or failure or embarrassing themselves or shitting the bed a few times'.

Failure is to be celebrated as an essential part of the pathway of progress. It is *on* the way to, not *in* the way of success as a learner and a manager.

Go forth, and allow your people and yourself to fail gloriously.

This is my favourite quote from boxing legend Muhammad Ali: 'Don't quit. Suffer now and live the rest of your life a champion.'

The keys to success are in doing a little each day to advance success for the rest of your life. If you want a strong resilient mind ready for life's challenges, you need to train it. The approach is the same whether you are training your mind or your body. If you start running today and decide to run a marathon tomorrow, it usually doesn't go well.

If you hit a critical mental fitness challenge and you've not trained up your mind to deal with it, it usually doesn't go well either. So, a little each day is a great place to start.

My Mental Fitness Checklist

- List the people who report to you. For each person, what do you think of them, or say to them, when they make a mistake? Are you condemning the person or the behaviour? Are you open to people learning from their mistakes? How do you show it?

- When a failure occurs, do you handle it based on a continuous improvement program?

- What are your workers compensation premiums and have you taken steps to work out what it would take to reduce them?

- Identify your weaknesses when it comes to creating learning pathways for people.

Chapter 25
Look for the signs

This story is about how you can fix the problem if you know where to look. The tools for this are about creating an environment that nurtures high performance. We learned that if you see with new eyes, you'll find the signs.

Story: There's always a canary in the mine shaft

When Ben made this mistake, he thought he was going to die. Angry volts of electricity shot through his arm and his back and he couldn't even back off as he was working in a confined space.

What traumatised him even more was that his workmates *laughed* as he lay there in shock.

He was incredibly lucky to come out of it alive but the psychological trauma took its toll. Even after 12 months, he felt tense about returning to work because random things would trigger the mocking laughter of his workmates to echo in his mind.

Just before the incident, he thought his supervisor had told him over the radio to turn the power back on. So he did.

The workers compensation inquiry opened up a huge can of worms. Following a root cause analysis, it was found that this incident could have been prevented if simple protocols for working in a confined space were followed. But the supervisor who radioed the instruction was new, from another state, and had never been part of such protocols in his previous employment. And no-one thought to induct him on the specific safety protocols for the site.

This was an incident that could have been avoided had the organisation considered the supervisor's situation and sent him to a specific role and responsibilities course before he took charge of such high-risk work.

We're sure that the organisation never intended for this to happen, but sometimes failures are so spectacular they come with big consequences when things go wrong.

It took many weeks for the organisation to hand down a final written warning to the supervisor. That they wanted to fire the supervisor on the spot and that the co-workers laughed when Ben was electrocuted were just two of many signs that this workplace was not mentally fit.

When we equip managers to look for the right signs, they can do something about their organisation's mental fitness. Huge improvements can then be made on the frontline.

For example, we asked the managers of a fuel delivery business to observe which of their truck drivers were silent, and which talked a lot. Sure enough, both types showed signs of being mentally unfit. The middle ground is where mentally fit people sit—these people understand their voice matters while not talking shit all day.

The signs are already there, we just need to teach managers where to look. They are shocked when we point out stories like this, then relate it to workplace mental fitness. They instantly get it.

Employees tend to put their needs above the company's. What if you connected the two and helped them realise those needs are not opposing?

It is almost impossible to be successful if you haven't first identified the sources of low mental fitness. Any change management project that you start without first getting this right is like shooting at the sky and expecting to hit the target right in front of you.

Toolkit

It's all about a mattering climate. Some organisations run so lean and have such high expectations of their people, who are literally running to keep up with their roles, that they miss being able to see what goes on around them.

To become an ace at spotting warning signs:

- Create a mattering climate. If people don't matter at your workplace then this book is not for you.

- Train as many people as you can on root cause analysis, so a good spread of people can see what the real reasons were when something bad happened.

- Understand that root cause analysis will tell you the facts every time.

- If people run so fast to keep up with activity at your workplace they will never be able to see the little things that are going wrong every day. This needs a solution.

- Look for ways to build better capacity in your people to cope with high-risk, high-demand environments.

- Do not use mentally unfit labour hire agencies because you may just be getting a bum on a seat that does not think and creates more hassle than they're worth.

- Find a way to make one hour per day of continuous improvement time available to frontline managers to focus on the critical tasks that people keep failing in.

- Start a continuous improvement group.

- Talk with your insurance company regarding what they think you need to do to lower your premiums.

- All of these items or similar ones will be found in a mentally fit workplace, so consider a program like ours that will help you to get past this obstacle.

Insights

When your people feel heard and valued, it can change what they think of the workplace. Creating a mattering climate makes a difference.

When managers engage their workforce with trust and respect, their people feel more empowered and inspired to create goodwill, collaborate better, and advance in personal growth and professional development.

We must learn to look for more ways to get people involved in creating productivity, efficiency and quality. Sometimes it means planting seeds of wisdom within the team and letting these grow into ideas. I remember a maintenance supervisor who gave each of his team ownership of tasks for shutdown work, from 12 weeks out through to completion of the shutdown. They were involved in planning meetings, allocating resources and supervising tasks. Talk about ownership, pride and motivation! It was all happening here.

Spreading ownership to the lowest levels possible can help your organisation Link:Flow:Grow, but you must be able to keep the discipline of productivity at high levels. It takes some thought and strategy, but when it works, it works really well.

My Mental Fitness Checklist

- If you use a labour hire agency, assess how mentally fit or unfit their recruitment process is.

- Ensure your people are trained to use root cause analysis to work on practical issues.

- In what ways could you implement a visible continuous improvement program?

- Do your leaders display mentoring or coaching capabilities? Find out what their subordinates think.

Chapter 26

Fast cars and ninja warriors

This story is about how shit makes great fertiliser for your mental fitness garden. The tools used are focusing on connecting with people to shift negativity. The insights are that it's okay to fail, but don't let it fester in the Failure bucket.

Story: The silver lining in your shitstorm cloud

Kris here. I've dreamt of the day since I was a junior manager: 'Someday, I'll have my dream car in my driveway when I'm celebrating my entry into senior management. To share and celebrate with my wife.'

It had arrived.

A customised black beauty that was shipped in from Germany. It was sleek. It was shiny. It had everything the way we wanted it.

It was ours.

The key felt right at home in my hand. Oh, the alluring click of the solid door as I opened it. The satisfying thump of it closing.

We breathed in the giddy scent of new leather seats. We surrendered our bodies to the luxuriousness. Giggled like teenagers in the backseat of a car for the first time.

Oh, the pride I felt firing up the ignition. Bringing this purring panther to life.

'Where should we go?'

'Anywhere. We can go anywhere!'

We agreed it would be an occasion befitting champagne and oysters. We cruised into the car park of the local gourmet supermarket and liquor store.

I saw it happen in slow motion out of the corner of my left eye. A moron in a maroon Mercedes reversing out of their parking lot right into ...

No ... No ... NO! *CRUNCH.*

To say I was upset was a bit of an understatement. My eye started to twitch.

I was proud that I didn't give the driver a piece of my mind. Not even when they revealed that they were on their mobile when backing out of the parking lot and didn't check their rearview mirror. Thanks to my internal mental fitness muscles, my expression of anger was controlled; not too terrible.

The insurance sorted it out. Peace was restored. Back on the road again. But we never got round to getting that champagne.

The extreme frustrations in life are a good thing!

Each emotionally charged situation gives you an opportunity to develop your skill of remaining mentally fit.

Perhaps you can relate this to many situations in your work day, whether it be safety failures, operational stupidity, someone sending an email that makes you furious, or even someone not saying good morning.

What's the key to navigating a negative situation in the workplace? Be mindful of the negativity already present. Accept that it is nasty.

Yes, this can be very hard to deal with. Take a deep breath.

How do you make it easier?

Remind yourself that your key objective is getting back to work and being successful.

Toolkit

To make rich fertiliser out of shit that happens in the workplace:

- Use your IOC audit to understand in depth what the real issues are. Make the program resonate due to known metrics and measures of success.

- Interview every key stakeholder to find out what they think.

- Gap assess them against a benchmark standard.

- Build relationships and acceptance.

- Look past the negativity and see the sunshine. Don't let it get you down. See their negativity as your fuel for change. Remember negativity is natural but only damaging if the culture does not tackle it head on. If the negativity persists the program is on a slow roll to failure.

- Look for the talent in the rank and field to nurture as step-ups to higher supervisory or managerial positions.

- Provide constant feedback, even when there is nothing to say.

- Use your non-negotiables to keep the honesty in the journey.

- Hold people accountable.

- Be firm on your expectations in a kind way.

Insights

Only the most focused, courageous and persistent leaders can transform a mentally unfit workplace into a mentally fit one. Why rob yourself of the fun and phenomenal satisfaction?

It's 'game on', workplace ninja warrior.

Be prepared for the negativity you shall battle to get there because it can be everywhere, even places you'd never expect.

We are all too quick to criticise and slow to provide positive feedback, so be aware of that and be prepared to fight that negative tendency.

Regard every negative situation as a mental fitness workout.

Focus on achieving EveryBest. Mental fitness is about not *staying* in the Failure bucket.

When a work situation produces a negative outcome, move it to the Work Improvement bucket as soon as possible.

My Mental Fitness Checklist

- If workers don't agree with the way your business operates, identify what you could do about it and still be an effective leader.

- As a manager, are you giving mental fitness lip service? Challenge yourself to walk the talk more.

- If one of your workers has a role that is mentally unfit, restructure the role with mental fitness in mind.

- Identify which work groups have the most negativity lurking in their ranks.

- List what you can do to keep motivation high.

Chapter 27

Love the challenge, not the job

This story is about how choosing a job you love is overrated. The tools used are about putting your ear to the ground when redesigning jobs. The insights we share are that you'd be surprised what there is to love about your job.

Story: A love-hate work relationship

Stan hates his job.

For almost 30 years he has done shift work and put up with less-than-stellar leadership and that has culminated in him working to live.

At age 62, he can't see himself going anywhere else so he makes the most of hating where he works. But the man is so clever: when product is off spec he makes changes that even the metallurgists won't think of. His mission is to create a saleable product without any reprocessing of material. He likes to do a good job.

Stan is not like most of the others at his workplace because they neither like the challenge nor the job and do as little as possible to get by. Boy, does that drive him nuts. There is a lack of mental fitness in this workplace and certainly a lack of effective leadership that holds people accountable.

This environment creates a poor focus on quality and getting it right the first time. There is always off-spec material to reprocess and fires to fight. It would be a great site to implement a mental fitness program.

Toolkit

Making workplaces interesting and enjoyable is not always easy—and, as they say, you can't please all the people all the time. As a matter of fact, some people just can't seem to be grateful for anything, so let's look at our tips for creating a great and challenging place to work. Take the yin with the yang to create flow.

Investigate all the hated jobs in your work area and make sure they are evenly distributed. We have never been to a workplace and stopped the business from doing what it does.

Here's how you can ensure the show goes on:

- Create a job rotation roster.
- Interview every person and get their perspective.
- Collate your information and make a plan to do what is practicable and worthwhile.
- Meet often with your people to discuss ideas and ask for input.
- Meet with the detractors and listen to their concerns as some may be reasonable.

- Implement change over time. Monitor who receives it well and who doesn't, and tweak your strategies to get more success.

- Consider a set of non-negotiables and seek input into what they could be.

- Toughen up your leadership team to hold people accountable.

- Provide feedback on progress and bottlenecks.

Insights

Have you seen this joke on social media? 'If you don't love your job, take a home loan. You will start loving it. Take another loan, and you will start loving your boss too.'

Should you take a job you don't love? Should you stay in a job you don't love? Yes, you should.

You have probably come across the thinking that a successful person loves every part of their job. If you have never been jobless while having a family to feed and a mortgage to pay, you may not appreciate that having a job you don't love can be a blessing, not a curse.

When someone says they love their job, they are talking about parts of it, not all of it. By all means, choose a job you mostly love, yet be prepared to deal with the bits you hate as part of the package.

As a manager you will never create a perfect workplace, but we can take it as close as possible by doing what is practicable. After all your effort, there may be people who are never going to fit and may need to be moved on.

Good, consistent, reliable, happy people produce the best results, so that is what you have to strive for. In our case study above, a lot would be achieved with more disciplined leadership—at least that would make it fair on all involved and enhance the workplace mental fitness.

Perspective can make or break you. Let your good intentions be grounded in reality. Choose the perspective and course of action that help your Company, your Team and your Self (CTS) to thrive. Even in the most tumultuous or chaotic conditions.

My Mental Fitness Checklist

- Make a list of what you don't love about your job.

- Envision how differently you would work if you accepted the bits you don't like.

- What do you need to change for your job to be great?

- How might you go about implementing these changes?

- Do one thing a week to create more happiness in your team.

Chapter 28

The problem to every solution

This story is about how to spot where the true problem originates. The tools in dealing with this are mentally fit organisation design and training. The insights come from the discovery of the root of the problem.

Story: It's not out there

Mentally unfit employees and managers alike love to play the blame game.

Margaret never worked a happy day in her life. It was always just a job, and she hated every second of it. She'd complain about the work, her workmates, the customers.

Bill didn't like his job either. Those bastards at work couldn't do anything right. He stuck with it anyway, for 40 years.

John often gets calls from managers saying, 'Our workers comp premiums are rising. Come and fix our supervisors, they are not keeping up with expectations!'

Yeah, yeah yeah. We can teach, train, coach and educate our darndest but we can't make headway where the mindset and culture will not allow it.

One organisation sank $33 000 into training for 11 qualified supervisors, and still they could not reduce their alarmingly high safety incidents rate.

If you want to throw away your money too, then call in the trainers and let them loose on your people, without first addressing workplace mental fitness.

We really need to take stock of where we are in times of change and investigate deeper below the waterline of the failure iceberg. Really get an in-depth understanding of why the old techniques are just not doing it for us anymore.

That company's contract was on the line because they could not meet their safety and organisational KPIs. Their $33 000 in training was ineffective because the real problem was in the way work was being done.

We coached and trained and educated the supervisors but soon found that most were not capable of creating the changes necessary (they were the types who had a problem for every solution), so we had to manage out a number of them and promote some of the star step-ups from the ranks. We took supervision time from 11 out of 12 hours to 8 out of 12 hours and reduced safety incidents to almost zero.

It was the use of high-touch skills added onto the already well-developed high-concept skills that made the difference. These skills changes included assertiveness, innovation, self-leadership, new techniques, relationship-building, teamwork, mutual support and other mentally fit behaviours. These are what made the difference, not the training certificate. When a supervisor has the support to grow and use new skills, they will.

Toolkit

The world of modern business can be very tough, and clients can be brutal with their decisions regarding our livelihoods. In order to prosper in the current world of work we suggest adopting these practices that will make a difference to the way you do things:

- Understand the difference between old management of work and new leadership of teams.

- Create a mattering culture, one where every single player is treated as importantly as anyone else.

- Establish your non-negotiables and make them non-negotiable, not just words on paper.

- Toughen up your leadership team. They must be firm and decisive.

- Train, coach, educate and support every person.

- Share the business plan ideals and ask for help in getting them.

- Provide feedback regularly. Have one-on-ones with people more than monthly, especially when establishing a new team.

- Create some career progression and have succession plans in place.

- If there are no roles in your team, sell your stars to another, otherwise their shine may start to fade.

- Hire only those people who can read and follow procedure. They can have other talents as well, but without operational discipline you have nothing but chaos.

Insights

Those who are stuck in the old ways see everything as too hard. We have heard the 'It'll never work around here' types who just add time and frustration to the mix. The problem to every solution is people: we are not growing and developing the people who fit in the Conceptual Age, we are still battling the modern workplace with the old-school styles.[26]

Your mental fitness battery power can be topped up. What's the essence of looking after your mental health, and staying mentally fit and active?

Train, train, train. Our brain is neuroplastic. Use it or lose it.

My Mental Fitness Checklist

- If you have an issue with negative thinking in your workplace, identify how you can address it.

- Assess whether your business would benefit from new thinking, innovation and continuous improvement. Look into how to implement some.

- Assess whether your people are equipped with enough skills to engage and interact positively to help the business grow.

Chapter 29

Everyone relax ... except HR

This story is about an HR manager's visit to heaven and hell. The tools used are about developing organisational support. The insights are that you must fix your mental fitness gaps first.

Story: St Peter's HR encounter

A HR manager died and was greeted by St Peter at the Pearly Gates.

'Hmmm ... we're not quite sure what to do with you as we've never had one of your kind here before,' St Peter said, scratching his head. 'So you can spend one day in hell and one day in heaven, then decide where you want to go for eternity.'

St Peter escorted the HR manager into an elevator and sent her down into hell.

The doors to hell opened onto a beautiful golf course. She found many friends and past fellow executives at its country club bar, all smartly dressed, happy and cheering for her. They ran up to welcome her and were soon chatting fondly about old times.

They played a perfect round of golf, then enjoyed a superb steak and lobster dinner with champagne. She met the Devil (who was surprisingly rather nice) and had a wonderful night telling jokes and dancing.

Before she knew it, it was time to leave. Everyone shook her hand and waved goodbye as she stepped into the elevator. The elevator went back up to heaven where St Peter was waiting for her.

'Now it's time to spend a day in heaven,' he said.

The HR manager spent the next 24 hours lounging around on clouds, playing the harp and singing; it was almost as enjoyable as her day in hell.

At the day's end, St Peter returned. 'So,' he said, 'Do you choose heaven or hell?'

The woman thought for a second and replied, 'Well, heaven is lovely, but I had a far better time in hell. I choose hell.'

St Peter took her to the elevator again and she went back down to hell. When the doors opened, she found herself standing in a desolate wasteland covered in garbage. Her friends were dressed in rags, picking up rubbish and putting it into old sacks. The Devil approached and put his arm around her.

'I...I...don't understand,' stuttered the HR manager, 'The other day you had a golf course and a country club. We ate lobster, and we danced and had a wonderful time. Now it's just this horrible wasteland and everyone looks miserable.'

The Devil looked at her and smiled, 'Honey, the other day we were recruiting. Today, you're staff.'

We laugh, because we know every company does this, right?

How powerful would it be for the recruitment pitch to be congruent with the actual experience of working in an organisation? Certainly that would increase job satisfaction.

Between two large-scale Australian employee surveys conducted by the Fair Work Commission[27] and Survey Sampling International for SEEK Learning,[28] about 20 to 50 per cent of respondents were dissatisfied with their jobs.

If you want to improve employees' job satisfaction in your organisation and reap all its positive ripple effects, take a serious look at implementing Link:Flow:Grow.

Let's get more HR managers into heaven.

Toolkit

To create a workplace where people feel valued and love going to work:

- Benchmark your business against the best in your industry, and envision what your business would look like in five years.

- Evaluate your current skill sets against those that you will need to succeed with. You will need to make some changes.

- Ask HR for help in solving the problem and if necessary get a third or fourth opinion.

- Hire a Driver champion to drive the changes, skill the people and create the Link and Flow you need to succeed.

- Create a mattering culture. Notice this is being said over and over—do you create a culture where each unique human is important?

- Change out the people who will not make the journey's end.

- Look at better flexibility in your Industrial Relations and Employee Relations options.

- Get into workforce development plans that reflect the business's flow and growth.

- Update every job description to reflect the skills needed to Flow and Grow.

- Never take your finger off the pulse.

Insights

Make sure your new starters know that this is the place they want to be.

There shouldn't be an 'oh damn' moment once they feel they have exited the honeymoon phase and entered the trenches.

Build an induction and welcome pack that brings a new member into the organisation. Starting a new job is stressful on its own—don't add to it. Settle the newcomer and have them see and feel your wisdom. The look they give you when they realise 'this is my new work home' is priceless and you know you have a winner. Search for it and bring the best minds in; you will only be the best workplace with them.

Lastly for now, make damn sure you don't lose them; you don't want the best minds working for your competitors. A person with true value demands trust and respect. This means your business processes must match.

My Mental Fitness Checklist

- Review your recruitment practices either with a recruiter, HR professional or someone who has recently been through the process.

- How long has it been since your business had a radical change of direction and leadership? Does it need updating?

- Look at your workforce development plans and assess how well they integrate with your business vision and profits.

Conclusion

Thank you for exploring the journey from organisational mayhem to mental fitness with us.

The road to workplace mental fitness may be a path less travelled for now, but it's going to make all the difference. Join our hero's journey; we know how to get you to victory.

To wrap things up, we'd like to address mentors, myths and mental fitness expectations.

Mentors are the key to mental fitness

Every champion team has a coach. Every manager who desires to be a champion leader must have mentors.

I (Kris) have been lucky to meet many mentors in my career. Every manager and guidance figure fuelled my success. Everyone who has worked with me in some way helped me to be where I am and helped me write this book.

I cannot emphasise it enough: if you want to build mental fitness in your organisation, in your team, in yourself, you must have mental fitness mentors.

I would like to acknowledge a few of my mentors.

Former United States Navy captain D Michael Abrashoff (now known as Mike Abrashoff) has deeply influenced my management approach. I haven't met him yet, but I've been a fan from afar. I treasure his practical and insightful book *It's Your Ship: Management Techniques from the Best Damn Ship in the Navy*.

I ask everyone to read or listen to this book at the start of their organisational redesign journey to understand the basic expectations of the mental fitness quest. Abrashoff's storytelling is simple yet powerful. You can enjoy a good read for a few hours.

Another mentor of mine is Jim Murphy. He has been in business for more than 40 years. He has run many successful enterprises and still does. He gives me little nudges and tweaks to ensure my management journey stays on track. Jim's age and experience are critical to guiding ambitious wannabes like me.

The knowledge transfer from mentoring is priceless. It's important for businesses to make new roles in the future for senior managers. To prevent brain drain. To tap into their mental fitness wisdom, not just their technical expertise. Mentoring is an important way for mental fitness to be recognised and developed.

Like physical fitness, mental fitness can fluctuate according to how much you train it. To keep it at its optimum, let's make it part of every manager's role. At all levels of management. Because it can have a big impact on business performance.

Let's create mentoring relationships at work to build mental fitness. Let's not just leave it to develop by chance, or fluctuate unmanaged. Create a workplace culture that encourages mentoring conversations. Yes, particularly the difficult ones.

'Are you being realistic?' we can almost hear someone ask. We've been asked similar questions in person.

In our experience, everyone is keen to chat once the workplace culture is mentally fit. We're not talking about touchy-feely confessions while sitting in a circle around scented candles, holding hands singing 'Kumbaya'. We're talking about the manager's responsibility to keep communication channels open, and to bring out the best in their people and treat them like humans, not meat robots.

We're also not talking about revealing innermost childhood secrets while lying supine on a therapist's stuffed leather couch. We're talking about people feeling safe enough to reveal weaknesses and make mistakes, in an environment focused on solutions, not blame.

In a mentally *unfit* culture, if their honest feedback contains anything negative, the person is viewed negatively. In a mentally *fit* culture, if their honest feedback contains anything negative, the *situation* is viewed negatively, not the person.

This applies to managers bringing up honest negative feedback to workers, *and* workers bringing up honest negative feedback to managers.

In a mentally fit workplace, the manager and worker work together as a team to fix the problem. They collaborate instead of behave negatively towards the person (who could be the manager or worker).

In a mentally fit workplace people are not afraid to speak the truth. They trust that starting honest conversations results in positive outcomes, not negative ones.

They start with a positive attitude: everyone is doing their best and if that's not good enough, as a manager I figure out how to achieve that.

Instead of accusations and blaming, everyone regards each other with trust and respect. With the intention of achieving positive outcomes for them as well as success for the team and the business.

We urge everyone to consider the ideas in this book and apply them, no matter what your position is where you work. Bring it up for discussion.

To get things started, not everyone needs to be mentally fit. Only the mental fitness advocate and change maker, the Driver.

With our three-day Link:Flow:Grow audit, you can find out on the first day if there is a manager with Driver capabilities in your organisation. If not, use us as your external Driver while you find one.

Think of us as mental fitness scaffolding. Our greatest satisfaction is to help you create a thriving workplace culture with high mental fitness that you call your own.

Let's create a workplace where everyone can communicate honestly and takes mental fitness seriously.

Three myths of being a good manager

If I (Kris) could write a letter to my 25-year-old self, I'd include the following.

> Hello mate,
>
> Congratulations for snaring your first job in a great company.
>
> I know you have a strong and stubborn drive to do whatever it takes to succeed.
>
> You're not afraid to work hard. But work hard on the right things.
>
> Before you rise through the ranks of corporate management, be aware of the three widespread myths you will surely hear. Some well-meaning people will tell you these and not even realise they are myths.
>
> Basically, you'll be told that great managers are smart, busy, and good people. And you will believe it for many years. Let me save you the trouble by telling you right now.
>
> It's bullshit.

Myth #1: The 'smartest' people make the best managers

Yes, showing evidence that you have brains *is* part of success. It doesn't, however, guarantee that the smartest people with the best degrees from the best universities *will* be excellent managers of people, or even themselves. Moderately smart people can be excellent managers. How so?

Triangulating research from Harvard University, the Carnegie Foundation and Stanford Research Center, we've known for 100 years that '85 per cent of job success comes from having well-developed soft and people skills, and only 15 per cent of job success comes from technical skills and knowledge (hard skills)'.[29]

Soft skills are things such as critical thinking, communication, adaptability and collaboration. And mental fitness. I personally think 'soft' is a misnomer because soft skills require grit and gumption.

Take professional ballerinas. They look all soft and delicate outside but are a hundred times stronger and more flexible than you on the inside, with ankles and toes of steel.

Be a mental fitness ballerina. The pink tutu and tights are optional.

I leave you with the words of Netflix CEO Reed Hastings: 'Do not tolerate brilliant jerks. The cost to teamwork is too high.'

More importantly, don't be one.

Myth #2: Successful managers are always busy

Some of the best managers I've ever seen seem like they do nothing. How are they so in control?

You're more likely to meet the other type: the busy manager.

'Sorry (not sorry), I'm late because I was busy with such and such.'

When you pop into their office and ask, 'Have you got a minute?' they say, 'I'm busy, so tell me in one minute what you want to say.'

Being busy sounds important, doesn't it?

Nope. If you're always busy, you're incompetent. I've said this to managers who tell me they're busy. And yes, they get upset.

'No need to get upset—prove me wrong, and I'll apologise.'

Yes, you can provoke your people sometimes. For the purpose of improving productivity. You can do this without being an asshole. Remember Myth #1 and the importance of soft skills.

A well-timed provocation changes the psychology right through the business. After that they'll think about what they are going to say before they say it.

Don't use the word yourself. It's banned from my management vocabulary.

Replace 'busy' with 'useful and productive' and you'll see a cultural change that enables more work to get done.

A great manager shouldn't be so busy that you don't have time for employees. Make sure you make time for whoever knocks on your door.

Myth #3: A great manager is a good person

Suppose you are the new CEO of a company. You need to make a decision.

You find out that your CFO is someone you knew at university. You also find out that he is in charge of ten people, who are suffering because the CFO has no mental fitness as a leader. He's dictatorial, morale is low, and he's getting good but not great results.

If you sack the CFO, it will be a huge embarrassment and his ego and mental health will suffer. He'll also think you're heartless and a lousy friend.

If you keep him, his team continues to suffer.

So the tough yet humane decision for the greatest good? Sack him. It could get nasty. You, the new CEO, will probably be seen as the bad guy. But that's okay. Sometimes leaders have to take a hit for the greater good.

In the classic knowledge worker paradigm, KPIs are primarily financial. Mental fitness and bringing out the best in one's people are not part of a senior manager's report card. But they need to be if, as leaders of organisations, we're serious about doing our job well.

So, 25-year-old self, those are the myths about being an effective manager that I've busted for you. Don't blindly idolise lofty degrees, don't be busy, and be prepared to be the bad guy when your organisation needs pruning. You'll do it a world of good.

Mental fitness expectations

Let's revisit a very important point: workplace mental fitness can be seen as a 'nice-to-have', not a 'must-have', especially during times of financial insecurity. Your job as a mental fitness leader gets harder when individuals, teams or companies are in a state of financial worry.

During these times, taper your expectations accordingly, yet don't give up on your mental fitness activities such as mentoring, resilience training and such. It may seem to be a 'nice-to-have', but it is actually a 'must-have' that affects your organisation's capacity for handling stress and change.

***

Dear reader, thank you for journeying through the concepts and stories in this book with us.

We have explored new ways to transform mayhem to mental fitness in the workplace. You have caught glimpses of how we apply Link:Flow:Grow to establish mentally fit organisations.

You have listened patiently as we shared our pet peeves about what needs fixing in today's organisations to create workplaces with stronger job satisfaction, meaning, purpose and results.

And you have now made the MindFit link that will show you how to create a kickass workforce that achieves long-term business excellence.

We leave you with parting thoughts from the admirable author of *It's Your Ship*, Captain D Michael Abrashoff:

> Most obstacles that limit people's potential are set in motion by the leader and are rooted in his or her own fears, ego needs, and unproductive habits. When leaders explore deep within their thoughts and feelings in order to understand themselves, a transformation can take place.'

For more information on how the IOC can help to transform your people and organisational performance, connect with Kris on LinkedIn (Kristopher Harold, https://www.linkedin.com/in/kristopher-harold-83032a78/) and we'll take it from there.

Notes

1. PwC commissioned by BeyondBlue, National Mental Health Commission, and The Mentally Healthy Workplace Alliance (March 2014). 'Creating a mentally healthy workplace: Return on investment analysis'. Retrieved from https://www.headsup.org.au/docs/default-source/resources/beyondblue_workplaceroi_finalreport_may-2014.pdf

2. WorkCover WA (October 2016). 'Stress-related claims'. Retrieved from http://www.workcover.wa.gov.au/content/uploads/2016/11/Stress-Related.pdf

3. Minerals Council of Australia (February 2015). 'Submission to the Western Australian Government inquiry into mental health impacts of FIFO work arrangements'. Retrieved from http://www.minerals.org.au/file_upload/files/submissions/15_78_SUBMISSION_TO_THE_WA_GOVERNMENT_MENTAL_HEALTH_AND_FIFO_INQUIRY.pdf

4. Abrashoff, Mike. *It's Your Ship: Management Techniques from the Best Damn Ship in the Navy.* Grand Central Publishing, New York. Revised, updated edition 2012.

5. http://www.smartcaptech.com/

6. National Soft Skills Association (13 February 2015). 'The soft skills disconnect'. Retrieved from http://www.nationalsoftskills.org/the-soft-skills-disconnect/7/

7. PwC commissioned by BeyondBlue, National Mental Health Commission, and The Mentally Healthy Workplace Alliance (March 2014). 'Creating a mentally healthy workplace: Return on investment analysis'. Retrieved from https://www.headsup.org.au/docs/default-source/resources/beyondblue_workplaceroi_finalreport_may-2014.pdf

8. Safe Work Australia (May 2017). 'Mental health'. Retrieved from https://www.safeworkaustralia.gov.au/topic/mental-health

9. Reynolds, E. (21 April 2017). '"I didn't know how I got there": When burnout is the best thing that could happen'. News.com.au. Retrieved from http://www.news.com.au/lifestyle/health/mind/i-didnt-know-how-i-got-there-when-burnout-is-the-best-thing-that-could-happen/news-story/46cff33802e208e0c5edb280d013e252

10. Cassells, R. (2017). 'Happy workers: How satisfied are Australians at work?' Retrieved from http://mwah.live/wp-content/uploads/2017/04/mwah.-Curtin-Happy-Workers-report.pdf

11. PwC (March 2014). 'Creating a mentally healthy workplace: Return on investment analysis'. Retrieved from https://www.headsup.org.au/docs/default-source/resources/beyondblue_workplaceroi_finalreport_may-2014.pdf

12. Safe Work Australia. 'Work-related traumatic injury fatalities'. Retrieved from https://www.safeworkaustralia.gov.au/collection/work-related-traumatic-injury-fatalities

13. Positive Psychology Program (16 December 2016). 'Mihaly Csikszentmihalyi: All about flow & positive psychology'. Retrieved from https://positivepsychologyprogram.com/mihaly-csikszentmihalyi-father-of-flow/ (Pronunciation aid: 'Me high? Cheeks send me high!')

14. Kotter, John (Undated). 'The 8-Step process for leading change'. Retrieved from https://www.kotterinternational.com/8-steps-process-for-leading-change/

15. Johnson, Spencer (video dated September 2013). 'Who moved my cheese?' Full movie. Retrieved from https://www.youtube.com/watch?v=16hxCB1Dvd4

16. Pink, Daniel H. (2005). *A Whole New Mind: Why Right-brainers Will Rule the Future*. Riverhead Books, New York. Retrieved from http://www.danpink.com/books/whole-new-mind/

17. Sonoma website (January 2009). 'Daniel Goleman's five components of emotional intelligence'. Retrieved from https://web.sonoma.edu/users/s/swijtink/teaching/philosophy_101/paper1/goleman.htm

18. https://en.oxforddictionaries.com/definition/capital

19. Rose, Todd (2016). *The End of Average*. HarperOne, San Francisco. Retrieved from http://www.toddrose.com/endofaverage/

20. Pink, Daniel H. (2005). *A Whole New Mind: Why Right-brainers Will Rule the Future*. Riverhead Books, New York. Retrieved from http://www.danpink.com/books/whole-new-mind/

21. Herrmann, Ned (2016). 'What is whole brain thinking?' in Herrmann International. Retrieved from http://www.herrmann.com.au/what-is-whole-brain-thinking/

22. PwC (March 2014). 'Creating a mentally healthy workplace: Return on investment analysis'. Retrieved from https://www.headsup.org.au/docs/default-source/resources/beyondblue_workplaceroi_finalreport_may-2014.pdf

23. http://www.clickcolours.net/

24. Sepah, Dr Cameron (4 March 2017). 'Your company's culture is who you hire, fire, & promote: Part 1, the performance-values matrix'. Retrieved from https://worldpositive.com/your-companys-culture-is-who-you-hire-fire-and-promote-c69f84902983

25. Manson, Mark (8 January 2015). *The Subtle Art of Not Giving a F*ck*. HarperOne, San Francisco. Retrieved from https://markmanson.net/not-giving-a-fuck

26. Pink, Daniel H. (2005). *A Whole New Mind: Why Right-brainers Will Rule the Future*. Riverhead Books, New York. Retrieved from http://www.danpink.com/books/whole-new-mind/

27. Fair Work Commission (updated). 'Job satisfaction of employees'. Retrieved from https://www.fwc.gov.au/resources/research/australian-workplace-relations-study/first-findings-report/6-employee-experiences/job-satisfaction-employees

28. Huffpost (22 March 2016). 'Less than half of Aussies are happy with their job, according to survey'. Retrieved from http://www.huffingtonpost.com.au/2016/03/22/hate-my-job_n_9519688.html

29. National Soft Skills Association (13 February 2015). 'The soft skills disconnect'. Retrieved from www.nationalsoftskills.org/the-soft-skills-disconnect/

Index

segment header start